Drupal 7 Media

Integrate, implement, and extend rich media
resources such as images, videos, and audio
on your Drupal 7 website

Liran Tal

BIRMINGHAM - MUMBAI

Drupal 7 Media

First published: July 2013

Production Reference: 1180713

Published by Packt Publishing Ltd.
Livery Place
35 Livery Street
Birmingham B3 2PB, UK.

ISBN 978-1-84951-608-2

www.packtpub.com

Cover Image by Erol Staveley (erols@packtpub.com)

Credits

Author
Liran Tal

Reviewers
Srikanth AD
David Madar
Grigory Naumovets
Michael J. Ross
J.G Sivaji
Janez Urevc

Acquisition Editor
Joanne Fitzpatrick

Lead Technical Editor
Sweny Sukumaran

Technical Editors
Joyslita D'Souza
Mausam Kothari
Sampreshita Maheshwari
Menza Mathew
Zafeer Rais

Project Coordinator
Arshad Sopariwala

Proofreader
Amy Guest

Indexer
Hemangini Bari

Graphics
Abhinash Sahu

Production Coordinator
Shantanu Zagade

Cover Work
Shantanu Zagade

About the Author

Liran Tal is a leading software developer, an expert Linux engineer, and an avid supporter of the open source movement. In 2007, he redefined the network RADIUS management by establishing daloRADIUS, a world-recognized and industry-leading open source project.

Liran currently works at HP Software, leading the development team on a Drupal-based collaboration platform in HP's Live Network R&D group.

At HPLN, Liran plays a key role in system architecture design, shaping the technology strategy from planning and development to deployment and maintenance in HP's IaaS cloud. Acting as the technological focal point, he loves mentoring his team mates, providing a drive for better code methodology and seekout innovative solutions to support business strategies.

He graduated cum laude in his Bachelor of Business and Information Systems Analysis studies and enjoys spending time with his beloved wife and soul mate Tal, playing his guitar, hacking all things Linux, and continuously experimenting and contributing to open source projects.

About the Reviewers

Srikanth AD is a web developer who is passionate about developing and optimizing websites for better user experience and search engine visibility. He is particularly interested in adapting content management systems for developing structured and scalable websites.

Check out his portfolio at `http://srikanth.me`. Or feel free to get in touch with him on Twitter `@Srikanth_AD`.

David Madar is addicted to technology, which has also caught up his family. He has came from the mainframe systems, working many years in banking organizations.

He has over ten years of work experience in developing web applications and websites, as freelancer and as an employee in the leading companies.

He is currently employed at HP Software.

Grigory Naumovets lives in Kiev, Ukraine. His background includes a Ph.D. in Physics and Mathematics. Since 1996, he has been working as an IT consultant, an IT specialist, and an ICT coordinator for several international projects, and then also as a freelance web developer and webmaster. After trying several web content management systems, he started using Drupal CMS in 2007. Since then, he has developed, maintained, and supported a number of monolingual and multilingual websites powered by Drupal 5, 6, and 7. He takes an active part in the community of Ukrainian Drupalers.

Michael J. Ross creates custom websites for businesses and nonprofits, using Drupal and other leading web technologies. In addition, he writes technical articles and book reviews, of which more than 530 have been published in print and online. For this particular book, he did not perform copyediting, but instead provided input on its usage of Drupal. This is the fourth Drupal book for which he has done technical reviewing. Anyone in need of a new website can contact Michael at www.ross.ws.

I would like to thank my mom and dad, who have always been supportive of my personal and professional efforts.

J.G Sivaji graduated from college in the year 2009. He holds a bachelor's degree in Computer Science Engineering from Jaya Engineering College (affiliated to Anna University). He gave a start to his technical evangelism as a Google Summer of Code student in 2009. He worked on the Drupal quiz module to improve its features and fixed several bugs along with other developers. Since then he has been an active member, contributor to the community in terms of writing patches to core and maintaining contributed modules. Currently, he is playing the role of Technical Director at KnackForge.

A technical enthusiast and one among the group of directors and founders of an exciting Drupal startup, KnackForge Soft Solutions Pvt., Ltd., Sivaji's prime role is not only confined to be the Lead of the Drupal team, Chennai branch, but also to hold the accountability for customer relationship and internal quality management.

Sivaji has contributed to a couple of books published by Packt Publishing as a technical reviewer. The list includes *Drupal 7 Module Development*, *Drupal 7 Themes book*, and this book, *Drupal 7 Media*.

I would like to thank my colleagues at KnackForge for motivating, realizing, and helping me to bring out the best in me.

Janez Urevc is a Drupal engineer from Slovenia, EU. He has dedicated his life to free software and open source since high school. He graduated in the field of software development in the faculty of Computer and Information Sciences at University of Ljubljana. The topic of his bachelor thesis was implementation of Scrum methodology in a web development department of a bigger media company. He has been an active contributor to Drupal for a few years. He contributed to various contrib modules and Drupal 8 core (full list of his contributions can be found on `http://drupal.org/user/744628`).

Besides Drupal, he's passionate about almost everything connected to web, free software, Linux, and software development. He participated in Google Summer of code, 2011 and was a mentor in 2012. He is currently working at `Examiner.com`, probably the biggest Drupal site on the entire Web. In the past he worked for Delo, Slovenia's biggest daily newspaper, where he led development of a few of the biggest Drupal sites in the region.

He maintains a blog at `http://janezurevc.name`, where he writes about his work and life.

www.PacktPub.com

Support files, eBooks, discount offers and more

You might want to visit www.PacktPub.com for support files and downloads related to your book.

Did you know that Packt offers eBook versions of every book published, with PDF and ePub files available? You can upgrade to the eBook version at www.PacktPub.com and as a print book customer, you are entitled to a discount on the eBook copy. Get in touch with us at service@packtpub.com for more details.

At www.PacktPub.com, you can also read a collection of free technical articles, sign up for a range of free newsletters and receive exclusive discounts and offers on Packt books and eBooks.

http://PacktLib.PacktPub.com

Do you need instant solutions to your IT questions? PacktLib is Packt's online digital book library. Here, you can access, read and search across Packt's entire library of books.

Why Subscribe?

- Fully searchable across every book published by Packt
- Copy and paste, print and bookmark content
- On demand and accessible via web browser

Free Access for Packt account holders

If you have an account with Packt at www.PacktPub.com, you can use this to access PacktLib today and view nine entirely free books. Simply use your login credentials for immediate access.

To my father, Eli Tal, who set me on this path.

"Thank you for the inspiration, thank you for the smiles

All the unconditional love that carried me for miles

It carried me for miles

But most of all thank you for my life"

Table of Contents

Preface

Integrating images, video, and audio content on a Drupal site requires knowledge of appropriate community modules, and an understanding of how to configure and connect them properly. With the power of up-to-date technologies such as HTML5, responsive web design, and the best modules available in Drupal's ecosystem, we can create the best Drupal 7 media website.

Drupal 7 Media is a practical, hands-on guide that will introduce you to the basic structure of a Drupal site and guide you through the integration of images, videos, and audio content. Learn to leverage the most suitable community modules and up-to-date technology such as HTML5 to offer a great user experience through rich media content.

What this book covers

Chapter 1, Drupal's Building Blocks, serves as an introduction to the building blocks of Drupal's node structure. Starting with a bit of Drupal's history, we move on to Drupal's very basic and prominent node structure. You will be introduced to Drupal's administrator user interface, which will help you create your own Memo content type.

Chapter 2, Views, Blocks, and Themes, shows how to display content with the use of the Views module user interface, which enables us to create content listing quite easily. We then move on to the presentation layer of Drupal and learn how to create and position content elements (blocks) in the various positions (regions).

Chapter 3, Working with Images, dives into deep water and helps in creating our very own content type for a food recipe website. We learn about the prominent Media module and its extensive support for media resources such as providing a media library, and key integration with other modules such as the Media Gallery. We also discover the concept of text format profiles and the use of WYSIWYG editors.

Chapter 4, HTML5 in Drupal, covers the HTML5 spec, why the Web needs it, and how to make use of the spec to create cross-browser-compliant HTML code in Drupal. We also learn about the canvas feature of HTML5, and create a signature management web application.

Chapter 5, Video Capabilities, explores the myriad of options available to add videos media to our website. We will learn about integrating with third-party video hosting websites such as YouTube, and create a YouTube-like video sharing platform.

Chapter 6, Audio Capabilities, covers different ways of working with audio content. You will learn how to customize an audio presentation, utilize the abundance of metadata that is potentially stored in audio media, and tie it up with Drupal's content structure.

Chapter 7, Leveraging Other HTML5 Features, starts off by showing you how to enable RDF support in our Drupal's website. We also learn how to implement a graphical chart with the help of the Views user interface and custom code. We also touch upon advanced theming and responsive web design.

Chapter 8, Enhancing Media Content, reviews Drupal's media configuration and tools, which aid a site builder in enhancing media-related content. You will learn how to apply image manipulations and how to build your own effects. You will explore the use of Colorbox and Plupload modules. Finally, you will learn about the rating module that adds voting capabilities.

Chapter 9, Drupal 8 and Beyond, reviews the upcoming Drupal 8 release and the changes it is introducing. Many of these changes are architecture and software design related changes, such as configuration management, core framework refactoring, better layout, and general mobile-ready with built-in support for HTML5.

What you need for this book

Drupal 7 requires PHP 5.2.5 or higher to run the Drupal code. You will also need one of the following databases to run Drupal 7:

- MySQL version 5.0.15 or 5.1.30 or higher
- PostgreSQL 8.3 or later
- SQLite 3.4.2 or later

You can use Apache HTTP, Nginx, or Microsoft IIS for the web server.

We recommend you to use a GNU/Linux, Apache, MySQL, and PHP setup, also known as LAMP, for best performance and community support.

Who this book is for

If you are a Drupal site builder and you wish to spice up your web applications with rich media content, then this book is for you. A basic understanding of HTML, JavaScript, and basic PHP module development in Drupal would be helpful, but is not necessary.

Conventions

In this book, you will find a number of styles of text that distinguish between different kinds of information. Here are some examples of these styles, and an explanation of their meaning.

Code words in text, database table names, folder names, filenames, file extensions, pathnames, dummy URLs, user input, and Twitter handles are shown as follows: "To make sure we understand this style when we use it in other places we will name it `grayscale_thumbnail`."

A block of code is set as follows:

```
name = "Image Effect - Sepia"
description = "Adds a Sepia image effect to image styles"
core = 7.x
files[] = image_effect_sepia.module
```

When we wish to draw your attention to a particular part of a code block, the relevant lines or items are set in bold:

```
<h1
  property="dc:title" class="node-title" rel="nofollow">
  Live school show
</h1>
```

New terms and **important words** are shown in bold. Words that you see on the screen, in menus or dialog boxes for example, appear in the text like this: "For the display format, aside from the interactive icons option, the **Rating** and **Percentage** options are pretty straightforward."

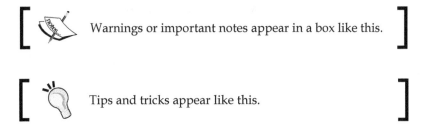

Warnings or important notes appear in a box like this.

Tips and tricks appear like this.

Reader feedback

Feedback from our readers is always welcome. Let us know what you think about this book—what you liked or may have disliked. Reader feedback is important for us to develop titles that you really get the most out of.

To send us general feedback, simply send an e-mail to feedback@packtpub.com, and mention the book title via the subject of your message.

If there is a topic that you have expertise in and you are interested in either writing or contributing to a book, see our author guide on www.packtpub.com/authors.

Customer support

Now that you are the proud owner of a Packt book, we have a number of things to help you to get the most from your purchase.

Downloading the example code

You can download the example code files for all Packt books you have purchased from your account at http://www.packtpub.com. If you purchased this book elsewhere, you can visit http://www.packtpub.com/support and register to have the files e-mailed directly to you.

Errata

Although we have taken every care to ensure the accuracy of our content, mistakes do happen. If you find a mistake in one of our books—maybe a mistake in the text or the code—we would be grateful if you would report this to us. By doing so, you can save other readers from frustration and help us improve subsequent versions of this book. If you find any errata, please report them by visiting http://www.packtpub.com/submit-errata, selecting your book, clicking on the **errata submission form** link, and entering the details of your errata. Once your errata are verified, your submission will be accepted and the errata will be uploaded on our website, or added to any list of existing errata, under the Errata section of that title. Any existing errata can be viewed by selecting your title from http://www.packtpub.com/support.

Piracy

Piracy of copyright material on the Internet is an ongoing problem across all media. At Packt, we take the protection of our copyright and licenses very seriously. If you come across any illegal copies of our works, in any form, on the Internet, please provide us with the location address or website name immediately so that we can pursue a remedy.

Please contact us at `copyright@packtpub.com` with a link to the suspected pirated material.

We appreciate your help in protecting our authors, and our ability to bring you valuable content.

Questions

You can contact us at `questions@packtpub.com` if you are having a problem with any aspect of the book, and we will do our best to address it.

1
Drupal's Building Blocks

Drupal is a free (licensed under the **General Public License (GNU)**, Version 2 or later), community-powered, open-source **Content Management System (CMS)**, which allows creating websites of many types. It's a great tool for both, users with no technical background, as well as top-notch developers, to use it for building complex websites and web applications.

Some examples for popular companies and organizations that decided to leverage Drupal as their content management system are FedEx, Symantec, MTV, and Duke University. The list is long, and you can find out more at http://drupal.org/case-studies or http://www.drupalshowcase.com.

In this chapter, we will cover:

- Nodes and Entities
- Creating custom content types
- Managing fields for content types

Drupal began back in 1999 with Dries Buytaert starting to develop his idea for a forum platform, and has greatly evolved into a leading and award-winning software. Since then, it has seen significant growth. Today, it powers millions of websites and has positioned itself as a candidate at the top of the list for websites and web platform frameworks. Drupal has a company behind it, Acquia, which drives for further cutting-edge development, keeping the pace with the technology trends, and serves as a commercial resource for those requiring professional services.

With almost every release, Drupal has managed to reinvent itself, for both its developer community as well as its users. With Drupal 7, it has even more transformed itself into a **Content Management Framework (CMF)**, by providing many abstractions to what content is and how it is handled. This road is setting the path for a large adoption by developers, to create web applications in many verticals, and has spurred a variety of platform niches from enterprise software, e-learning, and e-commerce, to social networking and collaboration software, to name a few.

Drupal 7's technology stack requires PHP5 (5.2.5 or higher) for the application server; MySQL (5.0.15 or 5.1.30 or higher) as the more favorable option for a database server, and HTML/jQuery for its presentation layer. The choice for this technology has no doubt helped in making it popular and easily deployable for hosting companies.

Nodes and entities

Being a CMS, in Drupal, most of your website probably will be structured around content. Whether it's managing it or displaying it in different layouts, themes, and views, content will be driving your website. Even more, content may be associated with the business logic about your website, which then defines a behavior based on content. Some examples for that may be, to send an email notification to users when a new content has been created, or to assign a rating system to content, such as five star rating or kudos, so that users can like it and in turn, this content receives higher visibility among your users. The possibilities are endless.

You have probably understood by now that content is very much a generic term for anything. It can be an article or blog if you're planning to run an online news-magazine website, or it may be a message post limited to 140 characters (if you didn't recognize, that's Twitter basically). Content can even be the posting of images by users, aligned in vertical columns with an infinite scroll, or the posting of videos. Throw into that the ability to rate, tag, create a personalized feed, maybe a customized bookmark/playlist too, then some of that special sauce we call social networking, by adding friendships and following the activity of other users in the website, and you've got yourself what we know today as Pinterest and YouTube.

Nodes

It's been a long time now that the term **node** has been at the very core of Drupal, so you have probably heard of it by now. As we've seen, content is very abstract and can take on many forms and shapes. Due to that reason, you'll often hear or read that "In Drupal, everything is a node" and that's most often the case. Whether your content is images, blogs, videos, forums, or polls, they all share very common characteristics and can be abstracted as a node.

These attributes of content such as title, body, created and modified time, whether the content may be commented on, and so on, are all pretty common properties across the different **content types**. And for this reason Drupal considers all these to be of the same nature, and so, to provide more flexibility without limiting the content types, it's simply called a node.

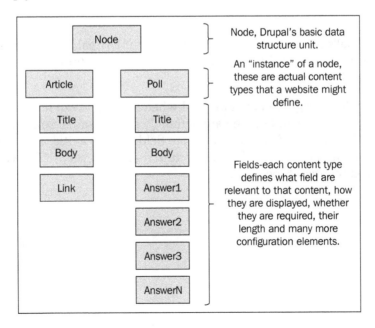

When examining specific content types in detail, it becomes clear that having a specific set of attributes such as **Title** and **Body**, is not enough. A **Poll** type content would require additional fields, such as text fields, which will represent possible answers. Download type content may require a file attachment field, in which a user can upload, and then another user can download. These additional fields have been developed as part of contributed modules, by the community, which answer this exact requirement of adding more fields and field types to nodes than what Drupal provides out of the box. You may have come to known these modules as **Content Construction Kit (CCK)** and **Chaos Tools** and many other modules which build upon this field's framework and further enrich content types. We will go into more details soon enough on this.

Out of the box, Drupal 7 ships with two basic content types: **Article** and **Basic page**.

The Article content type is used for blogs or news item, and as such it features properties such as, a comments area enabled, fields such as images and tags, displaying of the latest added content of this type in the front page. A Basic Page on the other hand doesn't have the comments area display, nor any special fields. Its display doesn't contain any information about the author who created the page and when it was created, but rather just prints the body of the page. It's easier to see the distinction between the two content types, and designing your content type's fields and settings is a very important part of building a website with Drupal.

Entities

Nodes are Drupal's term for any-kind-of-content, but Drupal 7 has taken a further step in abstraction and possibly coined a new phrase "everything is an entity", when introducing the entity model.

A thought may have triggered in your head when reading about nodes that while many content types are similar, they are definitely not the same. Some may not even require what Drupal would consider as a core field such as a title. This would then result in redundant data and a schema structure that is not very fit for what you had in mind for your content type to be.

To take this further, much inspired from other **Object Oriented Design (OOD)** concepts, Drupal also figured that it's basic schema for users and other objects such as taxonomy, comments, and so on, may be lacking too, meaning that it may be too strict, and site builders will eventually want to customize and extend those. With this thinking in mind, it has been made clear that nodes are not the only objects to take the even more generalized form of entities. This will rather extend to users and more objects that Drupal has been making extensive use of, for a while now, as its core building block (taxonomy, users, and comments, to name a few).

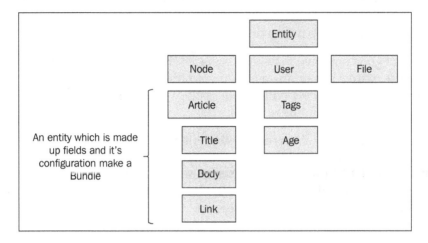

You may ask yourself what's new about defining entities because if you required your own unique data structure you could easily design the schema for it in your module's install file and decide what fields you need to create the database table that fits your needs. If you choose to go this road then those table fields are almost entirely disconnected from Drupal's built-in hooks system, and you are left on your own to tie them into Drupal's handlers. With Drupal's entity model you get this Drupal-awareness connectivity for free and many aspects of Drupal can then interact with your entities.

Entities allow us to create a common infrastructure across different objects, such as nodes and users. Then, if nodes are able to define a content type such as an article and assign fields to it, this goes the same for the users. This generalization of objects to a common ground provides software developers better maintenance and interoperability, and in result we, site builders, gain more features and powerful tools to customize and create the website as we see fit.

Bundle is the name given for the implementation of an entity type. If we implemented a node entity (meaning, we create a content type) and called it article, assigned some fields to it too, we inherently created a bundle called article. Bundles allow for the grouping of different entity types with their respective fields.

Nodes are not gone nor have they been replaced. For most content types, where it makes sense to treat something as a content rather than an entity, should not be abused and one can definitely build on the node's generic structure design with the envisioned content type and its related fields.

Creating entities is a task which requires defining many properties of it, whether it's fieldable, its basic fields structure, and so on. Sometimes, one would need to create an entity type which Drupal doesn't provide out of the box, like nodes or users, this process is much regarded as "further customization achievable by program code", hence requiring more in-depth knowledge and technical skills, which we will not pursue in the scope of this book.

Creating a content type

So far we've introduced the concept behind the entity model, and in specific, the nodes and their content types. Let's proceed by creating a new content type that we'll name **Memo** for keeping personal notes.

> What's so special about creating digital "stick it" notes? Even the simplest ideas can grow into great applications that can affect our everyday life. Evernote (http://www.evernote.com), which dubbed itself as "remember everything from saving thoughts and ideas, to preserving experiences" is the company behind the popular mobile and web app, for creating and sharing (rich media) notes with your peers, and is valued at an amazing $1B price tag.

We assume a fresh install of Drupal 7 (7.19 is the version available at the time of writing this book) so the first page should probably look as follows:

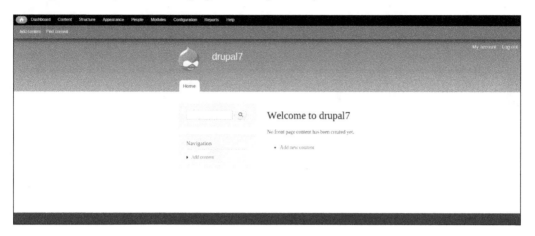

 When logged in as an administrator user you will see the administration navigation bar at the top in black color. We will often refer to this as the administrative navigation bar, mostly throughout this chapter, since we are just starting out. When otherwise navigation is being described, such as **Structure | Content types**, it is always referring to the menu items from that administrative navigation bar at the top. For your convenience, we will also often note in parenthesis the direct URL to access the relevant page.

To create the content type we can either make use of the shortcuts present in the page content area (this is the center of the page) or the **Navigation** block (in the left side of the page). If you are unable to locate neither of these we can use the administrative navigation bar at the top and navigate to **Structure | Content types | +Add content type** (`/admin/structure/types/add`).

In the new content type page, we'll provide the content type name, **Memo**, and an optional description.

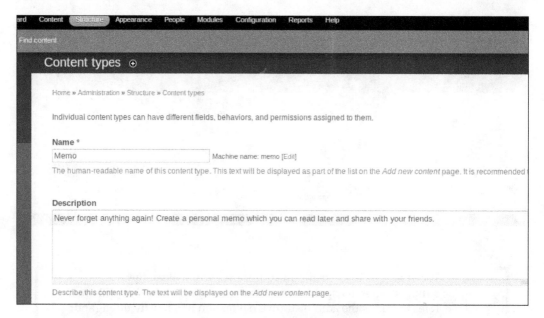

It's a better naming convention to use the singular word for a content type. As you can see, Drupal has already modified our title for its internal use, noted by the **Machine name** field.

More settings for this content type are available but we'll only customize the **Title** field name and call it **Memo**, leave the rest of the default options as they are, which basically are the same as Drupal's built-in Article content type which we described earlier.

Last, we will click on **Save content type** which saves the settings and submits the form.

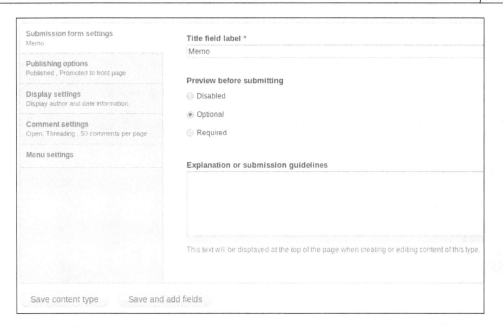

At this point, we have our newly created content type **Memo** and we can test how it works. We want to add content to the newly created **Memo** content type, so we will either use the shortcut for **Add content**, or if they are not present we can use the top administrative bar and navigate to **Content | Add content** (/node/add).

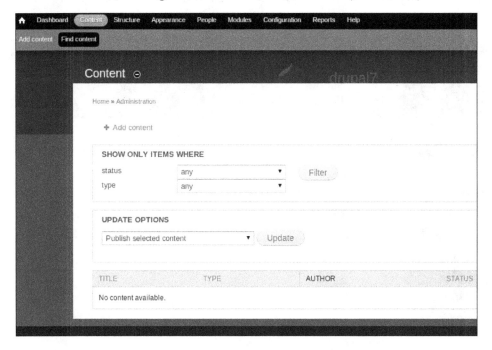

In addition to Drupal's default content types we see our new **Memo** content type.

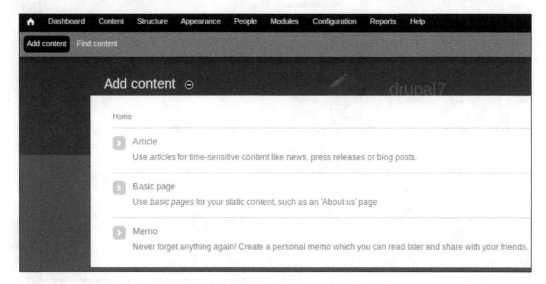

After choosing **Memo**, we will see the **Add content** form for creating our specific content type, where we will provide the memo title and a more descriptive body message.

Once finished with the memo we'll hit the **Save** button to submit and create our new memo.

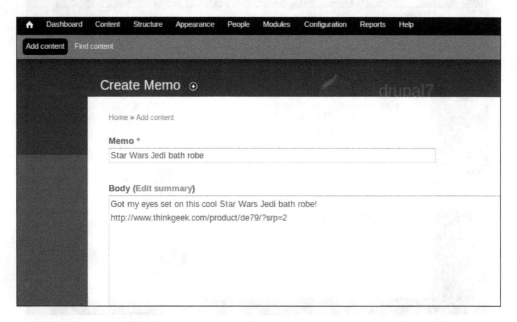

Our memo has been submitted and for logged-in users, it looks as follows:

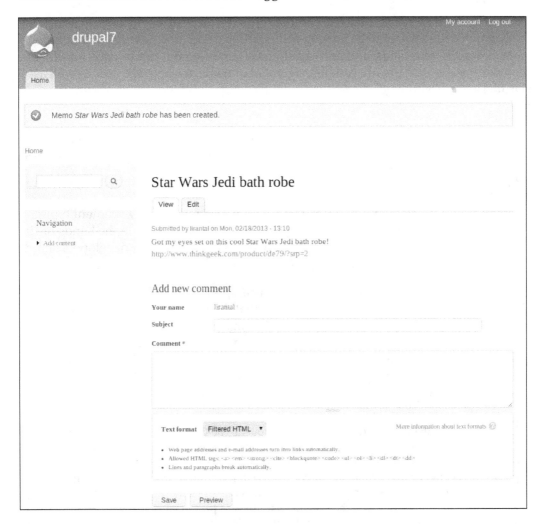

When looking at the preceding submitted memo, you may realize that there is room for improvements, such as, adding some images would have been more appealing to the eye. Also, it may be nice to have dedicated links field so that we can display them the way that we choose to, like a resources listing of them, at the bottom of the memo.

This brings us to our next topic in this chapter: **Fields**.

Fields

With fields, we can customize our content types to our pleasing, by adding select box dropdowns, file attachments, images, radio buttons, and more. Every content type may have different fields, and once a field has been created it can be used for other content types which greatly ease management of fields, for both the user as well as Drupal's inner working.

> We can attach fields to any entity, whether it's a node content type like an Article, or the user entity. As we mentioned before, the grouping of an entity type and its fields create a bundle.

Community powered module, CCK, has really helped revolutionize content types by providing flexible field types, field widgets, validation, and more, in the hands of site builders. This great effort did not go unnoticed from Drupal's core developers and it has been introduced in Drupal 7 as part of its core and the fieldable entity concept.

If you are coming with prior Drupal experience, specifically versions prior to Drupal 7, then you are most probably aware that the need for content types to support additional custom fields is essential. It makes a perfect example for the open source development model of **scratching the itch** where the contributed set of CCK modules, which introduced the ability to create fields and attach them to Drupal's content types, had found itself being a core component in many Drupal installations, and has long been a great tool in a site builder's arsenal.

> Scratching the itch is the #1 guideline of The Cathedral and the Bazaar (http://en.wikipedia.org/wiki/The_Cathedral_and_the_Bazaar) essay, in regards to the development models and methods in open source. This guideline relates to a scenario, where due to a rising need for something that is missing in a piece of software (like a feature, or maybe a bug in the system) a solution is produced in many forms by the community. Whether a developer decides to start his own project to address that requirement, or perhaps contributes a patch to add this requirement, this new functionality was introduced to an "itch" that the said developer had and wanted to fix it.

Adding fields to Memo

Let's add some fields to our memo content type.

Using the top administrative bar, navigate to **Structure | Content types**
(/admin/structure/types).

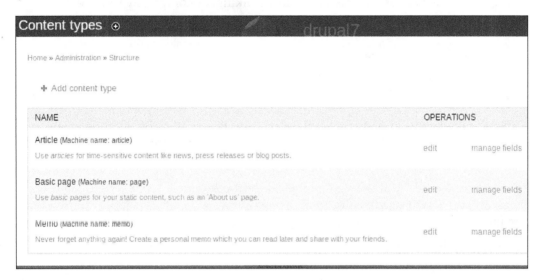

Out of the possible operations we are interested in, is the **manage fields** option,
so we'll click on that for the **Memo** content type.

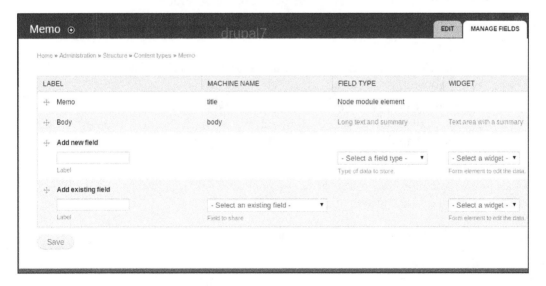

In this page we are now made aware, more than ever, of the fieldability of Drupal's node's content types. The **Memo** content type that we created has a **title** and **body** field (which you can tell by the **MACHINE NAME** column) and it doesn't come by any surprise as we've already set those when creating it. Yet, notice that the **title** field is an inherent field that is provided by the node entity, and we can't remove it, unlike the body field which we can customize to our liking, or completely remove it.

 Drupal as a CMS truly has one of the most flexible architecture design and allows developers who are proficient with its internals to really make (almost) anything happen, including making that **title** field "go away" if required.

Other than the fields already present, we can add fields either by defining a new field type and selecting its widget, or choosing a field type that was already created before, in this case it's Drupal's **field_image** and **field_tags**.

We'll continue with adding two more fields for the **Memo** content type: **Images** and **Tags**, and we can utilize the already existing options and set their label, starting with the image field:

After clicking on the **Save** button, we are presented with the **field_image** type's settings which we can customize to our needs, some of which are:

- **Allowed file extensions**: By default the permitted file types are .png, .gif, .jpg, and .jpeg.

- **Maximum upload size**: If we want to enforce it so that our hosting space is not abused.

- **Number of values**: By default set to **1**, this setting defines how many instances of this field will be allowed. For example, setting it to **Unlimited** will enable an AJAX user interface for adding more and more images when creating a memo.

Once you're satisfied with the settings click on **Save settings** button and we'll continue with adding the second **Tags** field:

The curious of us will notice that there are several widgets to use, for this field, which define the rendered view for each field when editing content: **Autocomplete term widget (tagging)**, **Check boxes / radio buttons**, and a **Select list**. This is where we need to put some thinking, **tags** (in Drupal this concept is referred to as taxonomy) have characteristics of being free form, and as such may grow to very big sets, which does not scale well with checkbox/radio HTML elements; and it's a very poor **User Experience (UX)** practice, if utilizing large items for a select box, so the **Autocomplete term widget (tagging)** option seems to be the most reasonable one, for a widget.

After saving, we're being presented with the **FIELD SETTINGS** page and we can notice how the settings for this field are very different from the previous image field. One particular setting that is set by default is the **Number of values** option which is set to **Unlimited** and it makes some sense with the use of tags as well as with our selection of the autocomplete widget.

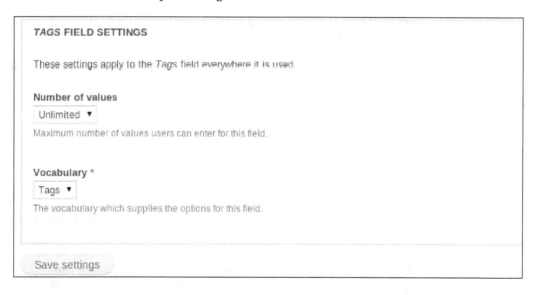

Also, notice how the **Vocabulary** option had also been set by Drupal. A bit on taxonomy in Drupal, also broadly known as **Tags**, is a core Drupal module which allows you to classify and organize data around your site. When should one use taxonomy, and not a field? When hierarchical structure is required, data needs to be kept as plain text. The vocabulary word comes from the concept of grouping a set of terms (this is what Drupal calls tags) together. Moreover, with the entity model in Drupal, taxonomy is an entity too, like nodes and users, which as you probably guessed right, allows us to attach fields to vocabularies.

Let's add another field to store links that we may want to add in our memos. Since links are really plain text, we can use the **Text** field type and its default (and only) widget is **Text field** too.

The default setting of 255 characters length limit is probably enough for most cases, including our purpose of this field for links, so we can leave it like that, and click on **Save field settings**. After which, we are then presented with the new text field's settings and we should probably change the **Number of values** option to **Unlimited** for this field too and click on **Save settings**.

Observing our new structure for the Memo content type we can see the newly added fields at the bottom of the list.

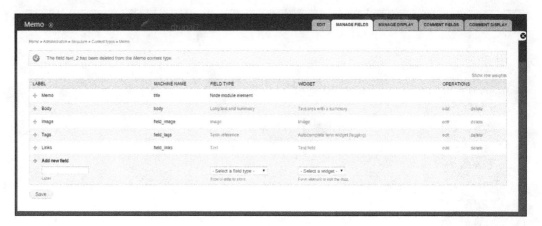

This listing also hints on the ordering of the fields, so if we wanted to make some changes there, such as bringing the **Tags** field beneath the **Memo** field, we can simply drag and drop this item by using the grey color arrow icon to the left of the label in the **LABEL** column. Once finished with reordering, we need to click on the **Save** button.

Adding a memo now will result in the following:

Viewing the form with our newly added fields looks as follows:

Configuring the Memo display

While the above fields' ordering dealt with managing the display of the form fields when adding or editing memos, we might also be interested in changing the overall appearance of an actual posted memo.

To do this we navigate to the **Memo** content type's configuration page again, which is at **Structure** | **Content types** | **Memo** | **manage display** (/admin/structure/ types/manage/memo/display), and we're presented with a new configuration page:

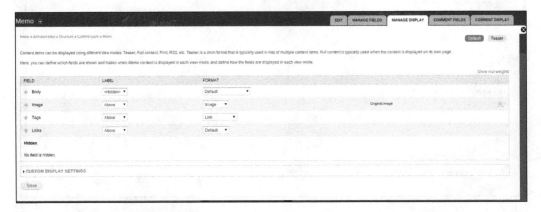

Displaying of content types may be different, depending on which view mode is being utilized. These view modes are for example, **Full content**, which is equivalent to the **Default** display mode for most purposes, and represents the mode for viewing the full page of the content type (this is for example, when in content listing, like in blogs, when you click on the "read more" link and view the full article on a dedicated page). Another view mode can be **Teaser**, which is often used when doing the content listing, similar to a blog, where you don't want to put too much content but rather a sort of summary for the content.

On the upper-right corner of the **MANAGE DISPLAY** configuration tab, we can see sub tabs for each view mode that we want to customize. By default, there's the **Default** and the **Teaser** mode. If we want to customize more view modes we can simply expand the **CUSTOM DISPLAY SETTINGS** link, choose any of the options there, and they will be added as subtabs.

Sticking with the **Default** view mode and taking a closer look at the fields table we can see the fields being used in this view (notice how all fields are being used, and none of them is hidden from the layout) and the **Label** and **Format** settings. The **Label** column configures where the field's label shows up, if at all, and the **Format** settings specify what kind of formatting rule to apply on the content that is being displayed for this field. If we examine the **Format** options for the **Body** field, then some options such as **Trimmed** or **Summary or trimmed**, makes sense for short content listings, like in the **Teaser** view mode that we mentioned.

There is definitely some room for improvements on the **Default** view mode for our memo, so here are some ideas for styling the view better:

We can remove the **Image** label next to the image as that's pretty self-explanatory, and put the **Tags** field at the top with the **LABEL** column displayed as **Inline**, to eat up less space.

> Instead of having the image laid out as its own field and space, in the view, we can put it inline to the text. Unfortunately, there's no Drupal way of doing this out-of-the-box function and this requires one of the many handlings, such as using the **Insert module** (http://drupal.org/project/insert) to put customized HTML image tags on the Body's WYSIWYG editor, or utilizing the **Media module** (http://drupal.org/project/media).

Once you're done setting up the field's display settings click on the **Save** button, and watch the new layout of your **Memo** content.

To practice on this, let's revive Drupal's front page node's listing. It uses the **Teaser** display mode, so we'll go ahead and update the fields listing. In the **Image** field, add a **<hidden>** label by drag-and-drop, and set the **Image style** dropdown to **thumbnail** by clicking on the gear icon, and setting the select box accordingly, then click on **Update**. And for **Tags**, drag and drop this field upwards as well, and set its **Label** to **Inline**. When done click on **Save** (feel free to further customize the teaser display mode to your liking), and view the home page to review your changes.

Summary

This chapter served as an introduction to the very building blocks of Drupal's node structure. Beginning from the very start, we have introduced Drupal's software stack, and tracked its origin back as an early open source project. We then continued to learn about Drupal's very basic and prominent node structure, which evolved in Drupal 7 and extended into powerful and abstract entities. Having created our own **Memo** content type, we have made acquaintances with Drupal's administrator user interface, which enables the site builders to build their custom content types, manage their fields as well as their display too.

In the next chapter, we will take a look at another aspect of Drupal's basic functionality, dealing with views, and the over-all presentation layer.

2
Views, Blocks, and Themes

After we covered the basics of Drupal's building blocks, nodes, and how is content handled in Drupal, we will learn about the presentation layer of a typical Drupal website and some of its essential components.

In this chapter, we will cover:

- The use of the Views module
- Understanding and making use of the blocks system
- Learning about themes and installing a new theme

Views

Up to this point we have discussed how content is structured, how are fields added to it, and even the actual styling of it's view and creating content.

An important aspect of working with content is not just about creating, editing, or deleting but also retrieving this content and displaying it as a list of items in many different styles (although do not confuse this with a content type's view modes).

Views, another powerful community-contributed module, aids in this task of providing an administrative user interface (UI) for building content listings, among many other tasks. If you have a little bit of database background then you can think of the Views module as a tool to create the SQL queries that retrieve and build content, which is exactly what Views is doing behind the scenes.

With Views you can create content listing as follows:

- Recent Memos that were created by users
- Reports about Memos used in your website
- Upcoming events mentioned in Memos

The Views module is one of tens of thousands of modules available to download, from the Drupal project homepage (`http://drupal.org`). While Drupal itself ships with some modules, these are considered core modules which provide very basic and essential functionality for Drupal websites to work (we can find these modules in Drupal's top level `/modules` directory). To extend this functionality, Drupal has been designed to be very modular and flexible so that community members can develop and contribute their own modules.

Installing the Views module

To begin, we'll need to first install the Views module. Navigate to `http://drupal.org/project/views`, scroll down and download the Drupal 7 version listed under **Recommended releases** option (at the time of writing this book, this was 7.x-3.5).

It is good practice to avoid mixing Drupal's core modules and contributed modules (or those of which you develop on your own). For this reason, you should unpack the archive in your contributed modules directory, which is in `sites/all/modules` directory of your Drupal's 7 install path.

Drupal 7 features a new way of installing modules and themes via the administrative interface itself. To make use of it, enable the Update Manager module in the Modules page (`/admin/modules`), after which you will see a new link at the top of that page to install modules just by providing it the URL for the direct download of the module or theme (which you usually grab from `http://drupal.org` module's page).

Views is dependent upon another module being present, the **Chaos Tool Suite** (also known as CTools), which is a developer's helper code module. If you don't have this module installed, then download it from `http://drupal.org/project/ctools` and extract it to the contributed modules directory too.

Navigate in the top administrative bar to **Modules** and scrolling down you'll see a new section called **View** with a couple of modules Views and Views UI. You can also notice the version detected for these modules as well as the useful information regarding the dependencies of this module, such as if this module requires other modules to be enabled. To continue, just toggle on the Views modules and click on **Save**. If any dependencies of the disabled modules have been found, you'll be asked to confirm enabling those modules so comply and then click on **Continue**.

The Views module, much like CCK, had a tremendous impact on Drupal and while attempts to add it to Drupal 7's core did not succeed it will be included in Drupal 8.

Adding a new Views

Views is now installed and we can start using it to configure content listing. Access it from the top administrative bar via **Structure** | **Views** (/admin/structure/views).

In the main Views page we see a listing of Views that were already created by default with the Views module but remain disabled, including a helpful description, tags to categorize and filter quickly through the list, the path to access a particular view, and the actions that we can perform; enable and edit, being the most common of them that we will work with.

 Installing the Advanced Help module will greatly help around when dealing with Views in specific, as well as other areas of Drupal.

At the top of the page we can also see more general actions to perform, out of which we care most about the **Add new view**, so let's click on it and continue with creating our first view as shown in the following screenshot:

Let's follow on how we filled the details for this view.

We've chosen helpful texts for the view name and it's description. Next, we decided what is our primary content type that we want to list. The select box features listing of users, comments or even files but we're interested in content in general, and specifically of type Memo. Notice how we can cherry-pick specific Memo content types that are tagged with one of the tags that have been submitted. Lastly on that row we see the sorting options.

Before we continue with the rest of this settings page let's recap on what vViews are all about. We have described the Views module as a tool for easily creating (complex) queries on the database and generating an output. What format is this output exactly? Views has a feature called Displays where it is able to create different kinds of outputs, depending on your needs. Some examples are as follows:

- **Page**: Probably the most common display mode, a page output represents an HTML page output. As such, a page has some settings unique for it like the URL path to access the page, the title that would be set, and can even integrate well with Drupal's menu system to also add a menu entry which will display this page view.

- **Block**: We will understand this topic very soon but we'll just point out that blocks represent components of information that can be placed anywhere in a theme. The Views module enables to generate actual blocks of content information.

- **RSS**: Turns your content listing into RSS feeds.

To continue, in the next configuration block we further refine the settings for the view that we are about to create.

We toggle on the page display and set the title, the path, and updated the **Display format** to **Unformatted list of fields**. By toggling the menu link option we added a menu entry for this page too. Let's finish by clicking on **Save & exit**.

Once we created a view and saved it, we'll be redirected to the Views page.

You can see how it looks now, taking notice of the path that was also created and the left-hand side menu entry to access **Recent Memos** as shown in the following screenshot:

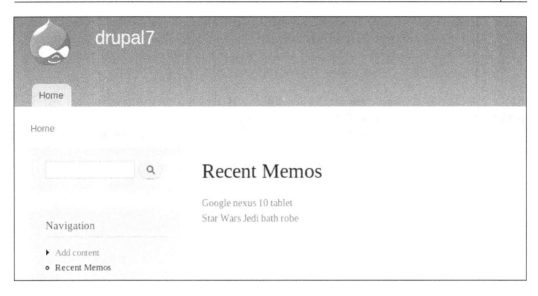

That listing is nice but it's very basic and we can probably add more information like who created each Memo, when was it and maybe add a little eye candy with attached images.

To edit the view go to **Structure | Views**, you'll notice the newly created **Recent Memos** fields at the top as an enabled view.

Drupal has support for contextual actions. Meaning that on every piece of content that the user is able to modify via a configuration interface you will see a gray gears icon with a down arrow which if you hover on will also create a border across the related object.

Interesting to note in this page that under the view name we also see more helpful information as follows:

- **Display mode**: We're seeing page as this is the only mode we've chosen for this view.

- **The source of the view**: Because we created this view from the user interface that the Views module provides, it will be saved to the database, which is why it says **In database**. The Views module exposes an **application programming interface** (**API**) which allows developers to create and manipulate views by writing code. If we had gone that road then it would have said **In code**.

- **Type**: The primary type of content that the view is based on. Content can be node content types, in which case that means actual content like our **Recent Memos** view, or it can also be a view that deals with users, for example showcasing a list of newly registered users.

In the operations we can click on the selected **edit** action to resume with our progress of editing the view. Once opened, the page may seem overwhelming with the amount of settings and configuration and indeed we can dedicate an entire book on the Views module to cover all of its features and capabilities (one book on this subject is Packt Publication's *Drupal 7 Views Cookbook* available at `http://www.packtpub.com/drupal-7-for-views-module-cookbook/book`).

We will logically break that views edit page into parts so that it will be easier for us to understand.

At the top we have on the left-hand side, the list of displays that are available in this view. The only display output is **Page** and it's also selected by default. We can click on the **Add** button and choose to add more displays like feeds or blocks but we won't do that now.

To the right we have a generic **actions** button to handle this view, for example to change the name, description and tags that were set for this view, or to perform more advanced actions like exporting or cloning the view as shown in the following screenshot:

At the bottom of the view we have an automatic preview generated for us every time we make some changes to the settings so that we can see what it looks like.

Specifically it shows general details such as the view's **Title** and **Path** in the mid of that section and beneath it the output page's title text and output content. It is also possible to debug the SQL query that is generated by the view by navigating to `/admin/structure/views/settings` and toggling on the option **Show the SQL query**, after which the SQL query will be displayed in the view editing page as shown in the following screenshot:

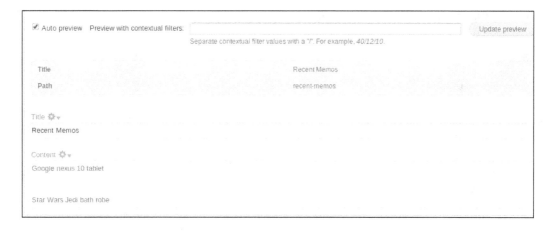

Concentrating on the very heart of the view's page settings, at this point, it looks like the following screenshot:

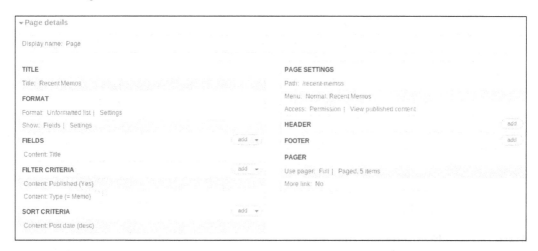

We will begin customizing our view by setting up the **FIELDS** section where the content's title is the only field and what we really want is to add a few more fields. In order to this, perform the following steps:

1. Click on the **add** button to the right of the **FIELDS** section.

2. In the opened dialog screen we can browse through the different fields and either use the **Search** text box or the **Filter** select box to focus on fields relevant to us. Out of that list toggle the following options:

   ° **Content: Image**

   ° **Content: Updated/commented date**

Once selected, click on **Apply**:

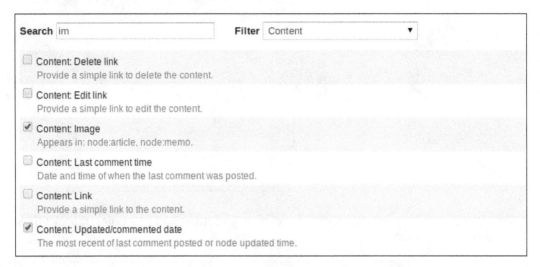

3. A configuration dialog screen will open now for each field we chose to add to further configure that field's settings:

    ◦ For the **Content: Image** field toggle off the **Create a label** setting and choose the thumbnail option for the **Image style** select box and finally click on **Apply**.

    ◦ For the **Content: Updated/commented date** field toggle off the **Create a label** setting and choose the **Time ago (with "ago" appended)** option for the **Date** format select box. We are now done so clicking on **Apply** for this last field will bring us back to the main views edit page.

We also want to add the username of the user who created each Memo but if you search on the listing of the possible fields to add you might have noticed that there is no such field. This is because our primary entity for this view is a (node) content type, hence there's no mentioning of users, comments or taxonomy. To pull in this further information we need to declare a relationship of other entities to the node's Memo content type.

Relationships are very much a representation of database's JOIN queries where a base table exists (this is our primary entity for the view) is joined against more tables (more entity types) which result in creating relationships, out of which we gain more fields to use.

To declare relationships, toggle the **Advanced** field set to the right of the page and click on the **add** button to the right of the **RELATIONSHIPS** section. We can now choose the **Content: Author** from that list and click on **Apply**, another relationship configuration dialog will display but the defaults there are fine. hence we'll click on **Apply** again as shown in the following screenshot:

By now we can open the fields option again and locate a field called **User: Name**.

In the field's configuration page we can clearly see that this field is a result of the author relationship we created. Let's set the label name to by and click on **Apply**.

Once we're satisfied with the collection of fields we can choose to rearrange their order by clicking on the down arrow on the **add** button of the **FIELDS** section and selecting **rearrange**. In the **Rearrange** fields dialog display let's set the image field at the bottom.

Most important part — to save this view's settings we need to click on the top right **Save** button and see how our content listing looks now:

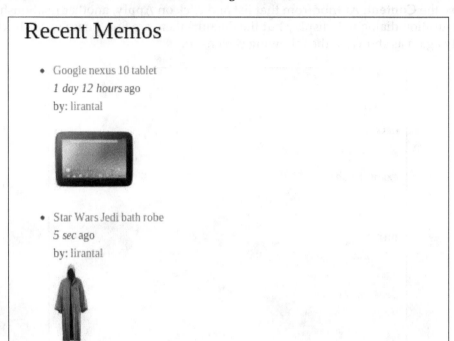

Views is very powerful and we have only scratched the very surface of it. In evidence of it's flexibility you can find many modules on Drupal.org that build on it more and more functionality and we will indeed re-visit some of them in the upcoming chapters.

Blocks and themes

Themes are a very important aspect of every website as they create the look and feel and are expected to convey a very intuitive and user friendly presentation of the underlying functionality.

Drupal's theme layer is very flexible and powerful, among many things it is composed from a collection of web assets like CSS, JavaScript, images, and of course the HTML template layouts.

Blocks

When looking at a website, it is often very common to notice a sort of pattern that emerges in the overall website's layout. Taking the US government's white house website (`http://whitehouse.gov`) for example, we can break it's layout into the following parts:

- The header which is at the top has to the left of it the White House's title, if so to say, along with a logo at the middle and some useful links to the right like contacting them
- The horizontal menu is the main navigation area of the website, right after the header line
- The middle top parts wins with image rich content and even wraps around a search area
- Then the main content area is divided into two columns, the left side has several blocks of content like popular topics and others beneath it and to the right of the content area there's an automatically updating feed of news, tweets and others as shown in the following screenshot:

In Drupal, these so called parts which we have just dissected, are called regions and have been introduced back in Drupal 4. They enable a site builder to place different kinds of content in the site's layout.

By the way, `whitehouse.gov` is a website powered by Drupal.

Understanding block regions

Let's look at our Drupal 7 site, can you tell which regions are used?

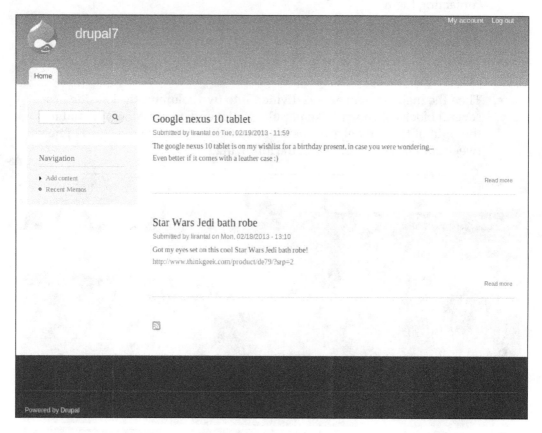

If you've identified at least the header, left side bar, right content area, and the bottom footer then you've done a great job!

As we've introduced themes before, they are very powerful, flexible, and possibly very different from one another. One of these differentiating aspects is the fact that each theme defines its own content regions and its main content area.

Blocks are Drupal's way of describing units of content and through the use of blocks we assign content to the different regions (you may also know blocks named as widgets for example in other frameworks but the concept is the same).

To understand which block regions are available for us, let's navigate using the top administrative bar to **Structure | Blocks** (/admin/structure/blocks) and the blocks settings page shows up. Click on the link **Demonstrate block regions (bartik)** at the top and you will now see the regions highlighted within the theme as shown in the following screenshot:

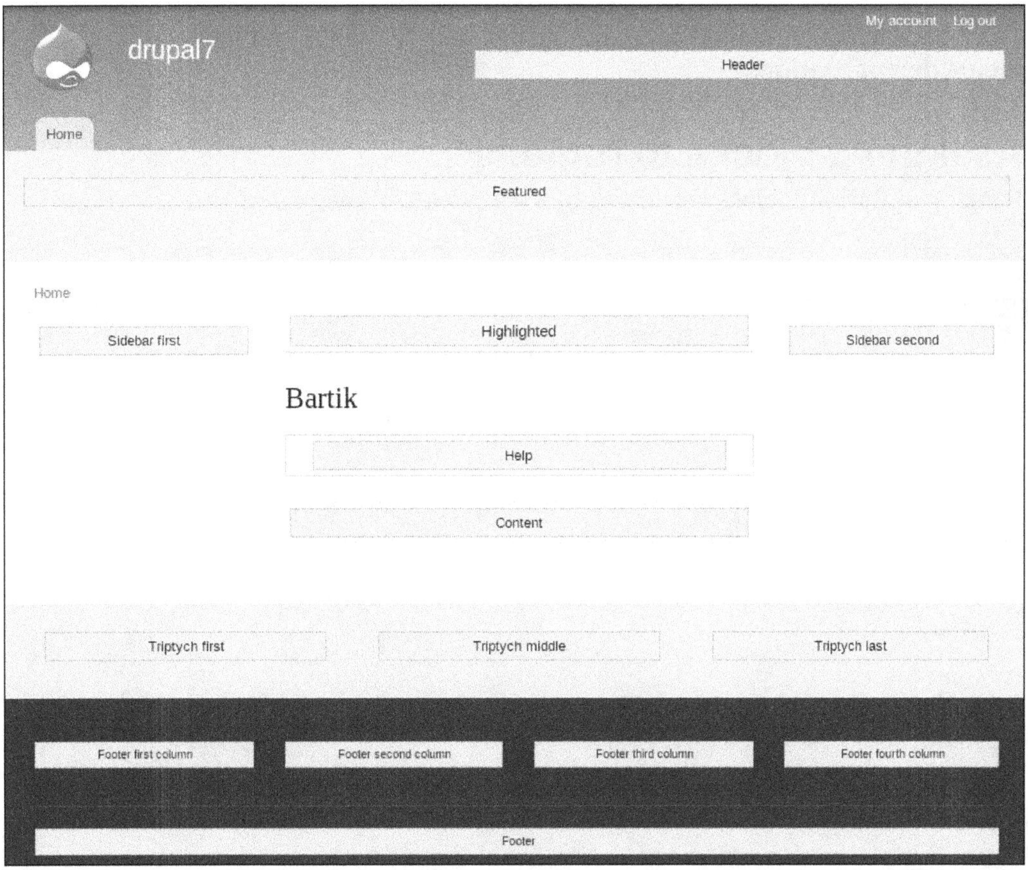

Only now, we realize the potential of the default theme. Some ideas to utilize these regions are as follows:

- Use the top **Featured** region for placing an image like the White House website's, or maybe even a full slideshow of images
- The three columns **Triptych** region can be used for placing contents of short blocks with images
- The four columns **Footer** area is commonly used for breaking apart the website's navigation into different sections

To go back to the blocks settings page click the top left link **Exit block region demonstration**.

Assigning blocks to regions

Looking at the main blocks settings page we can learn several things:

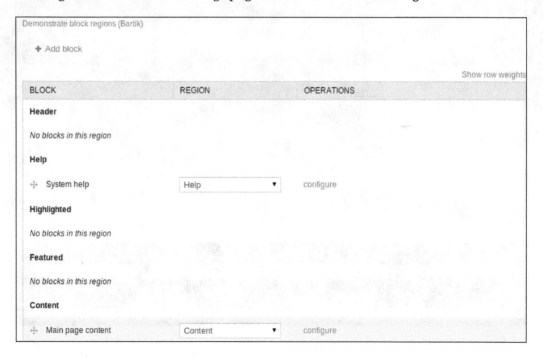

The top-right tabs of this page show the block settings for each enabled theme and the main page lists the available blocks and the regions they apply to. If we take a careful look we can see that the page is split, at the top there are all the regions listed with the enabled blocks in each of them, and at the very bottom of this table we see a list of disabled, yet more available blocks.

Let's go ahead and enable one of these blocks. **The Who's new** block sounds interesting so to enable and assign it to a region we'll choose one of the options, specifically the sidebar first option, from the select box in the **REGION** column. Upon choosing it the block has been immediately moved in the UI to the sidebar first region and should be visually noticeable using a highlighted bar. Moreover, let's reorder the blocks in that sidebar, as it contains more than one, and place our **Who's new** block at the top.

The blocks settings should look something like the following screenshot:

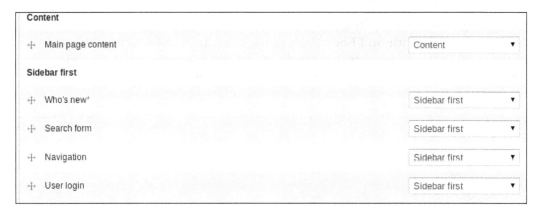

To finish we'll click on **Save blocks** at the bottom of the page and closing this configuration page we can immediately see the new block applied in our website's layout as shown in the following screenshot:

Creating blocks

Sources for these blocks may be many, such as other modules that we've downloaded and installed, which introduce new blocks content. Blocks themselves may have been created via programming code, or they may have been created by the Views module. It's even possible to create very generic and simple blocks through the user interface in the blocks settings.

We'll start by adding a static content block, for example, our contact information which is very common, and we can then place it in the footer.

Navigating to **Structure | Blocks** we'll click on the link for **Add a block** above the blocks listing. The **Title** and **Body** fields of the block are those which set the title of the block (if the theme chooses to make use of that in its presentation layout) and the body field is used to display the content for the block. Adding our contact information, it should look like as shown in the following screenshot:

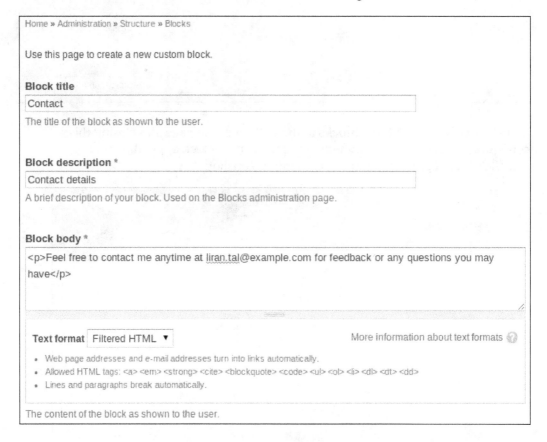

You may have noticed the **Text format** select-box which offers the filtered HTML as a default formatting. In later chapters we will learn how to use a rich text editor and then we'll be able to format the contents of this block better, such as adding a mailto address link and using bold or italic markup.

> It is possible to enable a PHP Filter module which adds the capability of hard-coding PHP code in the blocks content area (among other places as well) which seems to provide you with more dynamic content, although this method is often frowned upon and is not recommended due to many reasons, some of which are: mixing up programming code with the presentation layer, security aspects, managing of such code blocks inside Drupal's CMS, and internal database handling. Also, due to the fact that PHP code resides inside Drupal's logic this way (as opposed to being programmed using the module development facilities), it is being evaluated by Drupal on the fly which means that it does not get cached using OP Code caches like APC or others.

In the **REGION SETTINGS** we can set right there in the creation of the block page which region this block will show up on for each theme. The default theme shows up first and we'll choose the **Footer** option for that.

At last, we can fine tune who this block will be visible for in the **Visibility settings** field set, which adds the option to control who sees this block, and where with the following options:

- **Pages**: Defines either a whitelist (only the listed pages) or a blacklist (all pages except those listed) of page URLs, including the use of a wildcard character to control visibility

- **Content types**: When viewing a specific node content type, deciding whether to display this block or not

- **Roles**: Defines which roles this block content will be visible for

- **Users**: Provides the ability for users to configure whether they want this block visible or not, and the default visibility of this block for users which didn't yet customize this option

We will leave the defaults as they are (although feel free to experiment with this) which means that the block is always visible, to all users, in all pages. Once you're ready, click on **Save block** and return to the homepage to see the newly created block in the footer.

Themes

By default, Drupal 7 is shipped with several themes, out of which Bartik and Seven themes are enabled (if you're wondering why both are enabled we'll find out soon enough).

In essence, themes are a bundle of web assets like CSS and JavaScript but they also maintain their own settings, like regions which we learned about earlier. To find out which themes we have, as well as to configure their settings we'll navigate to **Appearance** (/admin/appearance) from the top administrative bar.

We can enable as many themes as we'd like and use them in different contexts. One use case for that is that Drupal 7 by default enables the Bartik theme as the default front-facing user theme and the Seven theme as the administrator's theme, which is the theme that you see when viewing administration pages (those popup dialogs which Drupal calls overlays). To change the administrative theme scroll to the bottom of the **Appearance** page and select a different theme.

While theme settings exist as site-wide default we can override these with each theme, depending on the provided theme's flexibility. To change the default Bartik theme we'll go ahead and click on it's **Settings** link in the **ENABLED THEMES** listing (or we can navigate via the tabbed interface and click on **Settings | Bartik**). as shown in the following screenshot:

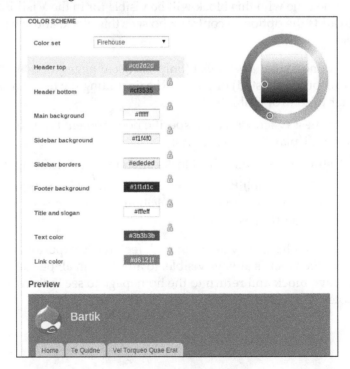

Some of Bartik's theme featured customizations are as follows:

- **Color set**: It provides a color theme to choose from. The previous screenshot shows the **Firehouse** option selected which already sets the preview as well as the different color elements of the theme already such as border, background, and text color.

- Toggling on/off the logo, site name, and site slogan. User pictures in posts and other themed elements which are reflected across the site's theme.

Themes for frameworks

Just like module development in Drupal has a common structure, so do themes. This structure organizes and streamlines theme development to create a solid ground for themers (theme developers) to further build and extend, much like in object-oriented programming.

Base themes, as they are called in Drupal, mandate such theme structure which enable developers to avoid starting from scratch and use a common convention to build on. This effort then results in what is known as sub-themes. By using sub-themes, developers can customize the site's look and feel and benefit from provided templates for nodes and blocks, re-using CSS classes, cross-browser compatibility, and more, all without breaking compatibility which will allow upgrading the base theme and stay up to date with current versions.

While it's possible to make use of base themes as the default site theme this is mostly not the case, nor the intention, but rather sub-themes are provided as default site theme and are required to be enabled along with the base theme.

Installing a new theme

Never let the defaults disappoint you. You're probably not really blown by Drupal's default theme and it's "sleek" user interface. That's ok, it's just a default out of tens of thousands out there for you to enjoy.

The official Drupal's website (`http://drupal.org/project/themes`) is one place to find your future theme, among many other free as well as paid resources on the Internet.

Zen, Omega, and a few other themes have made a name for themselves already as leading Drupal themes but you can find one more option, such as AdaptiveTheme, which became another great theme project aimed for modern HTML5 applications and responsive design.

AdaptiveTheme (`http://drupal.org/project/adaptivetheme`) is a base theme so enabling and setting it as the default theme is not enough and might actually break the UI. It has more than a few free, open source, and decent sub themes available and we'll go with Corolla (`http://drupal.org/project/corolla`). Download the latest recommended release of both of these themes (remember to match the minor version, that is, if you're downloading 7.x-3.x of AdaptiveTheme make sure to download the 7.x-3.x of Corolla too).

Once downloaded, unpack to `sites/all/themes` directory and navigate to **Appearance** settings, in which both themes should now be listed at the bottom with the rest of the disabled themes. Enable the theme called AT Core, and then click on **Enable** and set default for the Corolla theme. Then click on the **Settings** link for the Corolla theme.

As opposed to Bartik theme settings, Corolla's enormous settings page might be overwhelming to take all at once and shows how many theme tweaking options exist, especially with such professional and well-build themes. You can probably notice some interesting configuration options there like mobile related theming with the tablet and smartphone layouts. Even for the standard layout (which basically means a desktop browser resolution) we can define the columns sidebar positions and each column's width. We will visit many of these characteristics of modern HTML5 in following chapters.

While we can spend a week tweaking these layout options, for now we will configure images alignment in teaser view to show up to the left of text instead of having no alignment at all. You can find this option in the **Extensions** section under the **Image Settings** vertical tab and make this change. We're only making this change so we're done, click on the **Save Configuration** button at the bottom to visit your site's home page which should now resembles this screenshot:

Template engines

When presenting content, the actual content like a block or view's output is rendered into a template file (which may be wrapped by other template files).

In older days of PHP and web development in general, one could find program code and HTML markup together in one file which was bad practice in so many levels like separation of concerns, tightly coupling the view of a page with server-side code, harder maintenance and so on. Sometimes it's referred to as spaghetti-code but since then, design patterns and programming practices has evolved and methodologies like Model-View-Controller (MVC) have found themselves more and more employed by programmers and their frameworks and that goes for Drupal too. In turn, the presentation layer is indeed separated from the business logic and Drupal does it with the help of a PHP library called PHPTemplate which is shipped with it by default.

One of the values of using such MVC structure is that a developer who is working on writing a Drupal module can focus on the relevant programming without worrying how a block of content will be designed, which colors will be used etc, and the themer whose job is to work on styling the user interface can focus their work on CSS, JavaScript and HTML code for designing the website's look and feel and they can treat the underlying content with placeholder variables like $content without caring how this content is being produced (this is the developer's job).

Drupal's template engines are placed in `themes/engines` directory.

Summary

In this chapter we learned how to display content with the use of the Views module user interface which enables us to create content listing quite easily, without writing code, and without any knowledge of database.

We then moved on to the presentation layer of Drupal and learned how to create and position content elements (blocks) in the various positions (regions) which our theme allows for and even install a new theme of our choosing to introduce a completely new look and feel.

In the next chapter we will start working with the very first and primary media resources in websites, images. We will explore how to work with images on a Drupal website, such as embedding them correctly, managing image content across a website, and more.

3
Working with Images

It's time to begin with our very first and long-time media resource on the Internet — images. Images are not only a requirement that a site builder needs to meet according to some spec, but rather they should be thought of from the ground up when designing a website.

On the web, a picture really is worth a thousand words (if not more) as they contribute to a website's lively look and feel. Can you think of Facebook without images? **Instagram** is a billion dollar venture based solely on taking images and sharing them with your peers. **Pinterest** is another good example of taking a concept such as bookmarks, adding some eye-candy images to it, and there's another startup for you.

In this chapter we will cover:

- Adding image fields to custom content types
- Understanding the Media module for site-wide media resources management
- Installing and understanding the use of WYSIWYG and text formats
- Embedding images in content via WYSIWYG
- Creating image galleries, configuring them, and using them as blocks

Our theme content type for working with images in this chapter will be food recipes. Who knows? Maybe you can wrap your next venture based on this idea.

Because we have already learned in the previous chapter how to create new node's content types, how to add fields to them, and style the fields, we will not dwell into this again. Instead, I will show the new content type, called *rezepi*, which is a combination of the English word recipe and it's Polish translation przepis. Like it? That alone is probably worth a startup.

LABEL	MACHINE NAME	FIELD TYPE	WIDGET
⊹ Title	title	Node module element	
⊹ Recipe	body	Long text and summary	Text area with a summary
⊹ Course	field_course	List (text)	Select list
⊹ Cuisine	field_cuisine	List (text)	Select list
⊹ Difficulty	field_difficulty	List (text)	Select list
⊹ Ingredients	field_ingredients	Term reference	Autocomplete term widget (tagging)

The Media module

In previous versions of Drupal, the basic image field type didn't exist by default nor did another facet of image handling — the `Imagecache` module, which enabled the management of different image pre-sets (thumbnail, large, and so on). As we've seen with the `Memo` content type, this is no longer the case in Drupal 7, and at least a very basic support for images that already exist.

While there are many ways to build image integration into Drupal, they may all stem from different requirements and also each option should be carefully reviewed. Browsing around over 300 modules available in the Media category in Drupal's modules search for Drupal 7 (`http://drupal.org/project/modules`) may have you confused as to where to begin.

We'll take a look at the **Media** module (`http://drupal.org/project/media`) which was sponsored by companies such as Acquia, Palantir, and Advomatic and was created to provide a solid infrastructure and common APIs for working with media assets and images specifically.

To begin, download the 7.x-2.x version of the Media module (which is currently regarded as unstable but it is fairly different from 7.x-1.x which will be replaced soon enough) and unpack it to the `sites/all/modules` directory like we did before. The Media module also requires the **File entity** (`http://drupal.org/project/file_entity`) module to further extend how files are managed within Drupal by providing a `fieldable` file entity, display mods, and more. Use the 7.x-2.x unstable version for the File entity module too (as of the time of writing this book at least) and download and unpack as always.

To enable these modules navigate to the top administrative bar and click on **Modules**, scrolling to the bottom of the page we see the **Media** category with a collection of modules, toggle on all of them (Media field and Media Internet sources), and click on **Save configuration**.

Adding a media asset field

If you've noticed something missing in the rezepi content type fields earlier, you were right—what kind of recipes website would this be without some visual stimulation? Yes, we mean pictures!

To add a new field, navigate to **Structure | Content Types | rezepi | manage fields** (`/admin/structure/types/manage/rezepi/fields`). Name the new field `Picture` and choose **Image** as the `FIELD TYPE` and **Media file selector** for the `WIDGET` select box and click on **Save**. As always, we are about to configure the new field settings, but a step before that presents first global settings for this new field, which is okay to leave as they are, so we will continue, and click on **Save field settings**. In the general field settings most defaults are suitable, except we want to toggle on the **Required field** setting and make sure the **Allowed file extensions for uploaded files** setting lists at least some common image types, so set it to **PNG, GIF, JPG, JPEG**. Click on **Save settings** to finalize and we've updated the rezepi content type, so let's start using it.

When adding a rezepi, the form for filling up the fields should be similar to the following:

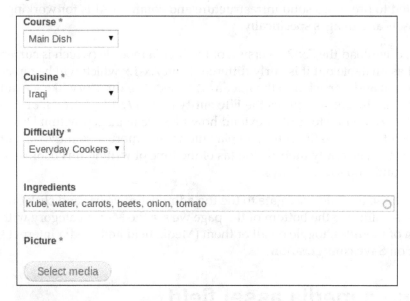

The **Picture** field we defined to use as an image no longer has a file upload form element but rather a button to **Select media**. Once clicked on it, we can observe multiple tabbed options:

For now, we are concerned only with the **Upload** tab and submit our picture for this rezepi entry. After browsing your local folder and uploading the file, upon clicking **Save** we are presented with the new media asset form:

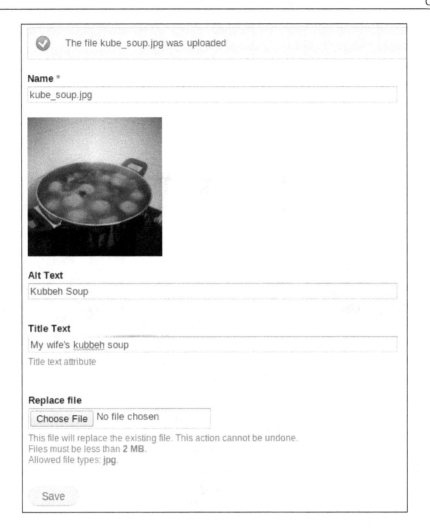

Our picture has been added to the website's media library and we can notice that it's no longer just a file upload somewhere, but rather it's a media asset with a thumbnail created and even has a way to configure the image HTML input element's attributes. We'll proceed with clicking on **Save** and once more on the **add new content** form too, to finalize this new rezepi submission.

The media library

To further explore the media asset tabs that we've seen before, we will edit the recently created rezepi entry and try to replace the previously uploaded picture with another.

In the node's edit form, click on the **Picture** field's **Select media** button and browse the **Library** tab which should resemble the following:

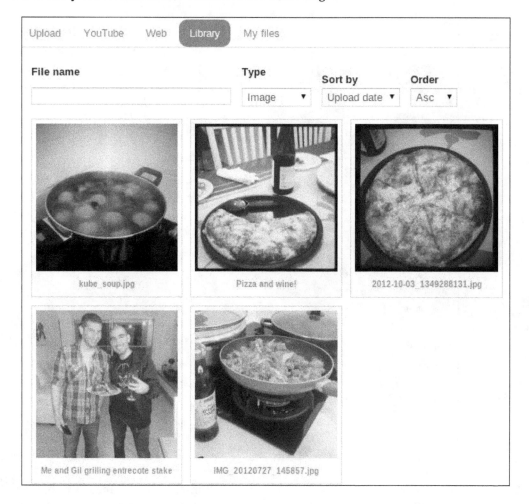

The **Library** tab is actually just a view (you can easily tell by the down-arrow and gear icons to the right of the screen) that lists all the files in your website. Furthermore, this view is equipped with some filters such as the filename, media type, and even sorting options.

Straight-away, we can notice that our picture for the rezepi that was created earlier shows up there which is because it has been added as a media asset to the library. We can choose to use it again in further content that we create in the website.

Without the media module and it's media assets management, we had to use the file field which only allowed to upload files to our content but never to re-use content that we, or other users, had created previously. Aside from possibly being annoying, this also meant that we had to duplicate files if we needed the same media file for more than one content type.

The numbered images probably belong to some of the themes that we experimented before and the last two files are the images we've uploaded to our memo content type. Because these files were not created when the Media module was installed, they lack some of the metadata entries which the Media module keeps to better organize media assets.

To manage our media library, we can click on **Content** from the top administrative bar which shows all content that has been created in your Drupal site. It features filtering and ordering of the columns to easily find content to moderate or investigate and even provides some bulk action updates on several content types.

More important, after enabling the Media module we have a new option to choose from in the top right tabs, along with **Content** and **Comments**, we now have **Files**.

The page lists all file uploads, both prior to the Media module as well as afterwards, and clearly states the relevant metadata such as media type, size, and the user who uploaded this file. We can also choose from **List** view or **Thumbnail** view using the top right tab options, which offers a nicer view and management of our content.

The media library management page also features option to add media assets right from this page using the **Add file** and **Import files** links. While we've already seen how adding a single media file works, adding a bunch of files is something new. The **Import files** option allows you to specify a directory on your web server which contains media files and import them all to your Drupal website.

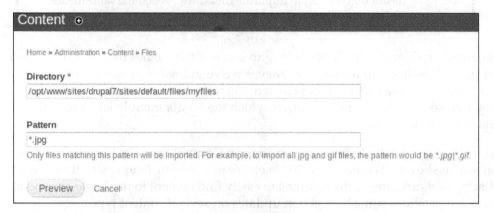

After clicking on **Preview**, it will list the full paths to the files that were detected and will ask you to confirm and thus continue with the import process. Once that's successfully completed, you can return to the files thumbnail view (`/admin/content/file/thumbnails`) and edit the imported files, possibly setting some title text or removing some entries.

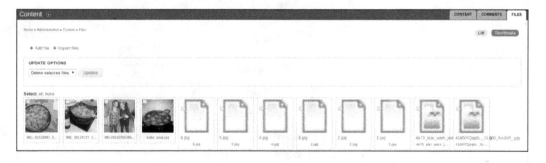

 You might be puzzled as to what's the point of importing media files directory from the server's web directory, after all, this would require one to have transferred the files there via FTP, SCP, or some other method, but definitely this is somewhat unconventional these days. Your hunch is correct, the import media is a nice to have feature but it's definitely not a replacement for bulk uploads of files from the web interface which Drupal should support and we will later on learn about adding this capability.

When using the media library to manage these files, you will probably ask yourself first, before deleting or replacing an image, where is it actually being used? For that reason, Drupal's internal file handling keeps track of which entity makes use of each file and the Media module exposes this information via the web interface for us.

Any information about a media asset is available in its **Edit** or **View** tabs, including where is it being used. Let's navigate through the media library to find the image we created previously for the rezepi entry and then click on **Edit** in the rightmost **OPERATIONS** column. In the **Edit** page, we can click on the **USAGE** tab at the top right of the page to get this information:

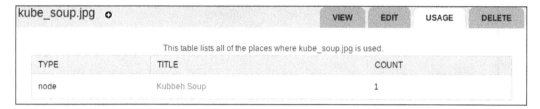

TYPE	TITLE	COUNT
node	Kubbeh Soup	1

We can tell which entity type is using this file, see the title of the node that it's being used for with a link to it, and finally the usage count.

Using URL aliases

If you are familiar with Drupal's internal URL aliases then you know that Drupal employs a convention of /node/<NID>[/ACTION], where NID is replaced by the node ID in the database and ACTION may be one of edit, view, or perhaps delete. To see this for yourself, you can click on one of the content items that we've previously created and when viewing it's full node display observe the URL in your browser's address bar. When working with media assets, we can employ the same URL alias convention for files too using the alias /file/<FID>[/ACTION]. For example, to see where the first file you've uploaded is being used, navigate in your browser to /file/1/usage.

Remote media assets

If we had wanted to replace the picture for this rezepi by specifying a link to an image that we've encountered in a website, maybe even our friend's personal blog, the only way to have done that without the Media module was to download it and upload using the file field's upload widget.

With the Media module, we can specify the link for an image hosted and provided by a remote resource using the **Web** tab. I've Googled some images and after finding my choice for a picture, I simply copy-and-paste the image link to the URL input text as follows:

After clicking on **Submit**, the image file will be downloaded to our website's files directory and the Media module will create the required metadata and present the picture's settings form before replacing our previous picture:

There are plenty of modules such as Media: Flickr (`http://drupal.org/project/media_flickr`) which extends on the Media module by providing integration with remote resources for images and even provides support for a Flickr's photoset or slideshow. Just to list a few other modules:

- Media: Tableau (`http://drupal.org/project/media_tableau`) for integrating with the Tableau analytics platform

- Media: Slideshare (`http://drupal.org/project/media_slideshare`) for integrating with presentations at Slideshare website

- Media: Dailymotion (`http://drupal.org/project/media_dailymotion`) for integrating with the Dailymotion videos sharing website

The only thing left for you is to download them from `http://drupal.org/modules` and start experimenting!

WYSIWYG

WYSIWYG stands for **What You See Is What You Get** and in the computer world this term is mostly associated with WYSIWYG editors. These are web based editors with support for text mark-up capabilities, such as bold, italic, underline, bullet points, and more, that transform an ordinary HTML text input into a rich text editor, such as Microsoft Word.

While it's possible to think of web applications that may not require WYSIWYG-like capabilities, it still is a prominent element in most Drupal sites for areas such as forums and blogs which makes it a desired component among site builders.

An example for a WYSIWYG editor (which we will learn more about later in this chapter) is the **CKEditor** library that aims to ease the creation of web content by enriching HTML text input with a tool-bar for text formatting.

Demo of CKEditor (`http://ckeditor.com`) in action for site content editors:

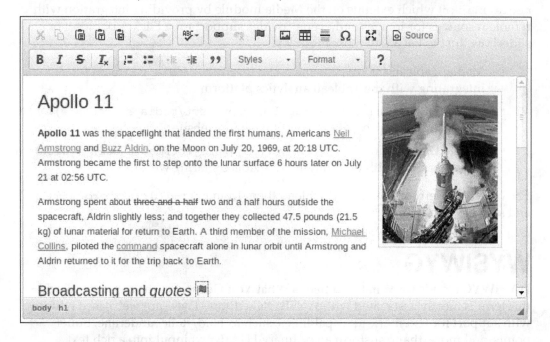

In regards to the WYSIWYG editor, taking a closer look at how our rezepi entry looks like, we can tell that the recipe **Body** field is pretty much a plain text entry lacking any mark-up:

This comes as no surprise due to how the recipe **Body** field looks like when we edited it and added content:

> **Recipe** *(Edit summary)*
>
> Mix the following:
> 4 beets, chopped to large pieces
> 2 onions
> 5 spoons of olive oil
> add salt, sugar, and pepper to your liking.
>
> Put it all in the pot and let it stew for an hour.
>
> **Text format** Filtered HTML ▼
>
> - Web page addresses and e-mail addresses turn into links automatically.
> - Allowed HTML tags: <a> <em> <strong> <cite> <blockquote> <code> <ul> <ol> <li> <dl> <dt> <dd>
> - Lines and paragraphs break automatically.
>
> Describe how to cook this dish. Be as descriptive as possible and provide step by step instructions for others to follow the recipe to it's perfection.

If you're paying a close attention to the recipe description field in the edit mode of the previous screenshot, you can notice a select box for choosing the text format for that input field. In case this had puzzled you before, we will cover this functionality next and how it ties up to the WYSIWYG support.

Text formats

Specially crafted user input may inject malicious data that will put your website in risk and may expose your users to threats. When dealing with user supplied text input, security actions must be taken to ensure that the provided input is not harmful. One way of attacking this problem is by filtering the user supplied input and allowing only a trusted set of characters. This is basically the essence of "never trust user input", a fundamental and important principle in software security.

Mitigating this security consideration, Drupal provides text formats (previously referred to as input filters) which define a set of filters that will be available for configured roles. Such filters may be used to specify a white list of HTML tags which form an allowed list of options, where anything not defined there is regarded as not allowed. For example, allowing the anchor tag (`<a>`) or the strong tag (`<strong>`) which are considered vital for users to share links and decorate their text in bold. Other filters may perform different kind of filtering task—instead of limiting tags, they may modify the user input completely. For example, an input filter may convert any line breaks that the user entered by pressing the *Return* key and turns them into an HTML `<br>` tag which creates breaks.

Drupal by default provides some text formats such as **Filtered HTML** and **Full HTML** which you've seen when working with long text input types such as the description fields. To review the settings for these text formats, we'll navigate to **Configuration | Text Formats** which shows the configuration page for the available text formats and the roles they are available for (`/admin/config/content/formats`):

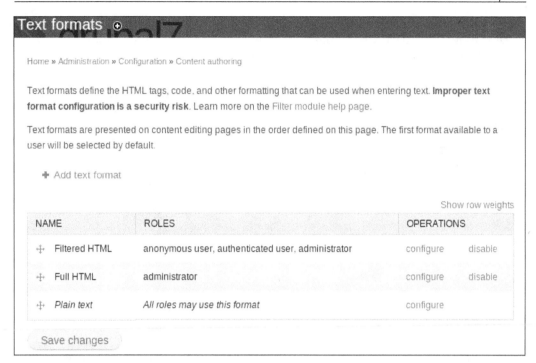

Except for adding a new text format and configuring or disabling the existing text formats, it is possible to control the default text format that will be set for users by using the drag-and-drop arrow icon and reordering the format options.

To understand why and how text is rendered into the view of some content when users save an input text which uses one of the input formats (like we did with the rezepi description field), we will edit the **Filtered HTML** text format. To view it's configuration, click on **configure** in the text formats list page (`/admin/config/content/formats/filtered_html`).

Roles which are allowed for this text format are by default all enabled roles, which Drupal supports out of the box and this makes sense too, because this is the **Filtered HTML** format which is supposed to be the safe type to let users use.

The filters that are enabled for this format comply with our definition for it—they mostly allow some basic functionality such as the first filter to allow limited set of HTML tags as well as modify the entered input and replace line breaks with actual HTML <br> tags for better readability.

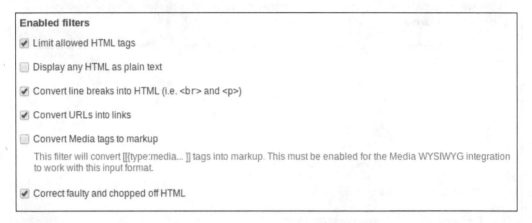

Due to the fact that filters tamper with the user input and modify the actual input, it is crucial to define which filters run first so that the user input isn't handed out "broken" for following text formats. For this reason, we can define the process ordering of the enabled filters:

Lastly, each filter may define its own settings to further fine-tune how the filter works.

For example, the filter for limiting the allowed HTML tags exposes this configuration setting to allow the site administrator to define the list of allowed tags and override the defaults for this filter.

In summary, the use of text formats enables us, as site administrators, to define the behavior of text rendering when user supplied data is typed-in to our input widgets. It is required to pay much attention to the configuration of text formats as improper settings may result in security vulnerability.

Adding a rich-text editor

There are many WYSIWYG libraries to choose from (FCKeditor, TinyMCE, YUI editor, and more) and Drupal allows for most popular of them to be plugged straight into it, yet you might find it difficult to choose the right one. It's a matter of preference as configuration and user interface differs, but also the roadmap and community around each library is quite important so we will follow best practices and work with the CKEditor library.

Drupal 8's WYSIWYG library of choice has been decided to be CKEditor according to Dries' announcement (`http://buytaert.net/from-aloha-to-ckeditor`) for many reasons, but probably mostly for its upcoming support for in-place editing which is a great UI for site content editors. So rest assured that the skills you've gained in this book with CKEditor as well as your user's experience will persist in your future upgrades with Drupal.

To provide flexibility with these third-party libraries we will make use of a base WYSIWYG module which acts as a bridge to connect Drupal's input widgets and any other library. First, we'll need to download and install this module's 7.x version (`http://drupal.org/project/wysiwyg`), followed by enabling this module from the modules page (`/admin/modules`).

Once this module is enabled, we can consult it's configuration page at **Configuration | Wysiwyg profiles** (`/admin/config/content/wysiwyg`).

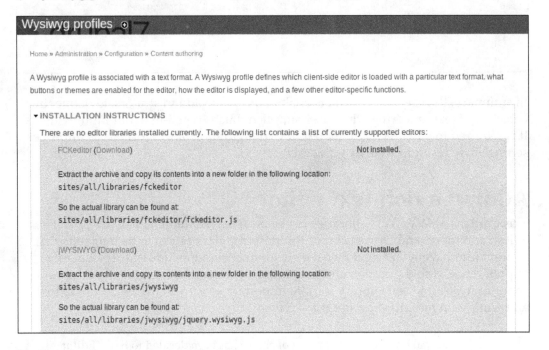

The page lists all the WYSIWYG editor libraries it supports with information of whether they are installed, where to download them, and how to install them. At the moment we have no library, so next it's required to download the CKEditor (or any other you've set your mind to) and place it in Drupal's root directory's `sites/all/libraries` which probably doesn't exist for you if you haven't done something similar before, so you will need to create it.

From CKEditor's website (`http://ckeditor.com/download/releases`), we will use Version 3.6.5 and not the latest version from the main download page. The reason for this is that at the time of writing this book, the WYSIWYG module had issues detecting versions of newer library versions.

After downloading and unpacking this library make sure that the following path exist in your Drupal's root directory: `sites/all/libraries/ckeditor/ckeditor.js`.

By now, you have installed all the WYSIWYG related components (the module and the library) and it is required to associate the CKEditor with one of the text formats that are available. If you are still on the **Wysiwyg profiles** page, simply reload this page otherwise navigate to it.

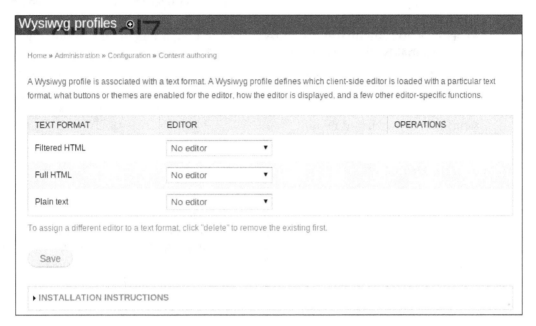

While it is possible to install and add to your Drupal site more than one WYSIWYG editor and configure different text formats and roles to use each one, it is not a common practice and unless there's good reason this is not advised.

There is a consideration to be made when deciding which text format to associate the CKEditor with. If we associate the CKEditor with the default **Filtered HTML**, only a tiny portion of the editor's functionality will be used because that format only allows a very limited set of HTML elements. It is tempting to associate the editor with the **Full HTML** format and really opening up support to most, if not all, of the editor's functionality but because by default that format is only available for the administrator role, it's not really helpful to the rest of your users. At this point you might consider changing the text format's role settings to allow your site users to make use of it too, but that will introduce major security threats to your website. Security threats such as embedding external JavaScript code using the `<script>` tag, embedding external resources with the `<iframe>` tag, or any type of cross-site scripting (also known as XSS attacks) will put your site and your users in harm's way.

To mitigate such security issue as well as provide good user experience, we can employ various configurations, here are some options:

- Use the **Filtered HTML** text format for members which will only use it for commenting on blogs and alike, where rich text support isn't really required. Create a new text format and assign the CKEditor to it for allowing rich text experience to content authors, but add allowed tag filters to only permit tags for functionality that is enabled through the CKEditor.

- Assign the CKEditor to the **Full HTML** text format, enabling fully functional rich text editor, but make sure the only roles who have access to this format are co-administrators or content authors which are part of the site's staff, hence, they are trusted people.

Other configurations may exist, especially with the help of extra modules which can be found on the Drupal site.

For the sake of demonstrating the WYSIWYG features and upcoming Media module capabilities, we will assign the CKEditor library to the **Full HTML** text format. To do that, select it as the editor from the dropdown list and click on **Save**. Removing an association is possible by clicking on the **Delete** link in the **OPERATIONS** column (this might be confusing but it's not going to delete the text formats, just the association). We'll proceed with configuring the editor by clicking on the **Edit** link.

There are many configuration options, grouped in their own field sets for easy administration, which enable better customizing level of the editor profile. The default settings are same for most options so we will focus on the areas which require the administrator's intervention the most.

The **BUTTONS AND PLUGINS** field-set is the crucial configuration which determines which functional buttons will be enabled and exposed to the user in the WYSIWYG editor. Let's go ahead and enable some of them, such as **Bold**, **Italic**, **Image**, **Link**, **Align left**, **Align right**, **Underline**, **Numbered list**, and others.

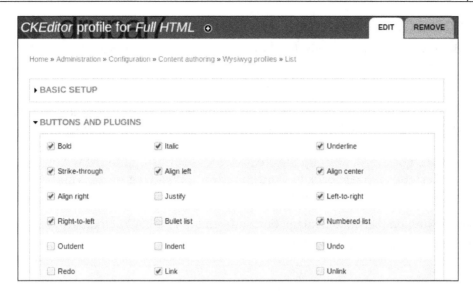

Once you're satisfied with the setup, save the profile settings and search for our previous rezepi entry and edit it. If the edit mode opened with the **Filtered HTML** text format as default, change it to **Full HTML** from the select box and the WYSIWYG editor will show up. This is the time to experiment with it and re-edit the recipe description.

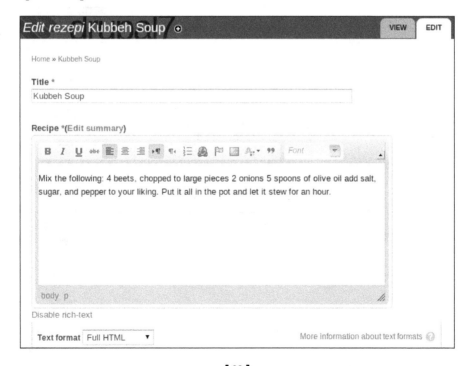

Embedding images in content

Providing content authors with the ability to add pictures to their posts is not a feature to underestimate. It is a vital feature that goes a long way and your users will appreciate a good user experience.

You might have noticed that the CKEditor configuration page featured a button for working with images in the **BUTTONS AND PLUGINS** field-set, where we toggled on some other buttons previously. If you have already enabled it just out of curiosity before, that's good (and keep up the creativity and curiosity thing, it will do you only good), otherwise navigate back to **Configuration | Wysiwyg profiles** and edit the **Full HTML** text format to toggle on the **Image** button and save these settings.

When clicking on the square **Image** button from the WYSIWYG toolbar, you should see the following pop-up dialog for adding an image:

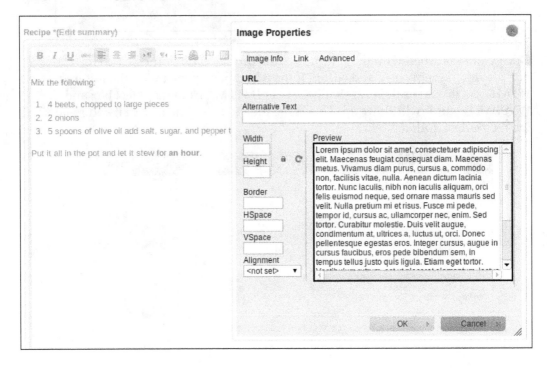

If you really liked the media library support that we earned with enabling the Media module then you surely may realize that the out-of-the-box support of CKEditor for adding images to content may have some shortcomings. The image popup itself is very configurable. By typing-in a link to an image resource on the Internet, the user immediately sees a preview and can further tweak the height and width, border, picture alignment verses text, specifying if the image will also be clickable, and even some advanced settings such as specifying a CSS class or an ID attribute. Still, one cannot wonder why are we required to always provide a URL address to add images? If these are internal links in your Drupal site then even a stronger argument is— why shouldn't we be able to browse them and reuse those files?

The Media module had already concluded that such a use case (of integrating with a WYSIWYG editor) will exist and for this purpose they created a filter that makes use of special media tags which the media browser plugin for the WYSIWYG editor will be using. All of these extensions and integrations are already provided by the Media module, the user just needs to enable them and configure accordingly.

The filter, which as we discussed earlier, is being used by text formats to define an allowed behaviour (or character set) and enforce user input security, for texts that are typed-in by the user. Due to the fact that we have chosen to work with the **Full HTML** text format for the WYSIWYG editor, we will need to edit it (`/admin/config/content/formats/full_html`) and toggle on the filter called **Convert Media tags to markup** to enable it, and then click on **Save**.

As far as the WYSIWYG editor settings are concerned, it's required to edit the desired profile (`/admin/config/content/wysiwyg/profile/full_html/edit`), in our case it's **Full HTML** which is bound to the CKEditor library, and in the **BUTTONS AND PLUGINS** field-set options toggle off the **Image** checkbox (if it was toggled on previously), toggle on the **Media browser** and click on **Save**. It's not strictly required to remove the **Image** button but it's probably desirable as we rather not confuse our users and provide them with very intuitive interface.

Even if you have worked before with the **Image** button for the CKEditor toolbar, by removing the **Image** button and adding the **Media browser** button the images being used in content that was already created will remain intact. Moreover, when users will edit their content and double-click their images in the WYSIWYG editor, the same **Image** button popup will appear and enable them to edit these settings.

When adding new content or editing an existing rezepi entry, you will now notice a new button to the right of the toolbar, which when clicked upon, will present the same popup dialog that the user have been using previously with the dedicated image field we added.

Try adding an image using the new media browser button on the toolbar and you will notice that after selecting an image which already exists in the library you are required to specify the display formatting for this file. Because we haven't yet configured display formatters for the different file types, the default format named **Default** is actually less suitable and will simply display a filename link to the picture. Instead, choose either **Teaser** or **Preview** and click on **Submit** to save your options and then click on **Save** to finish editing. Don't worry, we will cover managing file types and their display formats soon enough.

If it's required to further fine-tune image properties or reveal information on how the image will be used in terms of resolution and other aspects, it's possible to just right-click on the added image and choose **Image Properties** which will present CKEditor's image handling popup dialog, which you should already be accustomed to. This functionality is inherent to the CKEditor and doesn't depend on the **Image** or **Media browser** button that we enabled.

Image galleries

With image galleries as site builders, we would like to enable our users to create sets of images which are grouped together and can be viewed in a streamlined manner. There are many ways to present image galleries and many ways exist to approach the technical requirement. One example would be to reuse our knowledge of the **Views** module. To do it, we might need to create a new content type called **Picture Gallery**, or maybe a better name would be **Albums** (if that sounds familiar, it's because that's how the big social network players are calling it). For this content type, we will probably add fields such as title, description, dates for when these pictures were taken as well as location field for where the pictures were taken, and finally, an image field for file uploads which allows for unlimited instances of this field. Once we have the content type structure defined, we can create a new view to represent a grid view display of content nodes of this type. Further customization can then be applied and extended as we please though the example should suffice.

Enabling an image gallery feature

Just like the view module example, there are many modules in Drupal which enable such gallery functionality yet we will focus on the **Media Gallery** module which has been developed by Acquia, the same company that sponsored the creation of the Media module, which as we've seen is of high quality, integrated well, and builds on good flexibility and modularity concepts for future extensions of this functionality with other modules.

The Media Gallery module is still under heavy development (at the time of writing this book) so we will use it's 7.x-2.x-dev version (http://drupal.org/project/media_gallery). The Media Gallery also depends on other modules which we will need to download, unpack, and install too:

- **Multiform** (http://drupal.org/project/multiform) – This is a module which exposes API for developers to create multiple forms for Drupal to handle as a single form element.

- **Colorbox library** (http://colorpowered.com/colorbox) – This is a jQuery lightbox plugin which provides a popup dialog user interface to navigate through pictures. Note that Colorbox is a library, similar to the CKEditor library that we needed to install, so it should be unpacked into the sites/all/libraries directory. From their website download the latest version, referred to as master (respectively, the downloaded filename will probably be master.zip). After unpacking it, your directory name might be colorbox-master, if so, rename it to plain colorbox. By now you should have the directory sites/all/libraries/colorbox and the file sites/all/libraries/colorbox/jquery.colorbox.js. Unfortunately, due to the Media and Media Gallery's 7.x-2.x branch still being in development there are some bugs. One of which is that while the CSS file for displaying the Colorbox is being loaded from the sites/all/libraries/colorbox/ directory, the JavaScript file is loaded from the sites/all/libraries/colorbox/colorbox directory. The fix is quite simple, although not very elegant, and that is after unpacking the colorbox directory in the sites/all/libraries directory, copy the ZIP file and unpack it once more inside the sites/all/libraries/colorbox directory. To make sure you've followed this correctly, the end result should provide you with the following file paths: sites/all/libraries/colorbox/example1/colorbox.css and sites/all/libraries/colorbox/colorbox/jquery.colorbox-min.js.

It is possible and even likely that this bug might have been fixed by this book is published, in which case you can ignore creating the previous duplicate directory structure. After installing and enabling (from /admin/modules) all of these modules we are now ready to start using the gallery feature.

Creating an image gallery

The Media Gallery module created a new node content type called **Gallery**. To start creating a new gallery, we'll click on the **Add Content** from the top (`/node/add`) and click on the new **Gallery** option that appears in the list. The **Create Gallery** page that shows up now sets our new gallery settings, first of which, is its name and description:

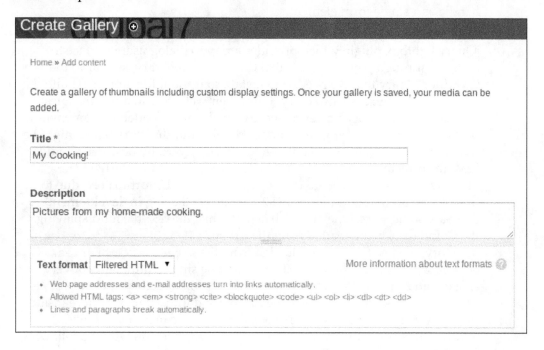

The behaviour of the gallery, it's presentation and other settings are administered in the **Gallery Settings** field-set:

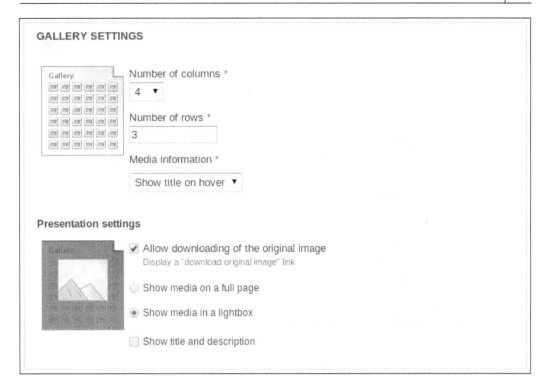

By specifying the **Number of columns** over **Number of rows**, we are actually affecting the layout of the media inside the gallery. The **Media information** select box defines whether the title of each media resource (our images) should be presented, and if so, where to place it—below the image or only show it as a tooltip when hovering over the image.

The presentation settings allow further refinement for how our images should be displayed:

- Allowing the download of the original image.

- Showing the media on a full page resembles a full node view (that is, node/<NID>) while showing the media in a lightbox means that once an image is clicked upon, it will open up in a popup dialog and allow navigation (back and forward) through the rest of the images in the gallery. The Colorbox library that we installed earlier comes to play in this feature—that's the meaning of the term lightbox.

- Showing the title and description will provide extra metadata on the lightbox popup dialog.

If we had chosen to show the media on full page, there's no meaning for this checkbox, as anyway the full page node view displays the title, description, and the rest of the fields for that content type, if any.

You will notice that if you click around in-between the presentation of the media style buttons, the left thumbnail will change to give you an idea of how it would look.

The defaults are very useful and are in-par with other popular web social networks so they are a safe bet to go with if you're unsure what would make a good user experience.

Go ahead and click on **Save** and you should now see your gallery view, although it's empty of any media resources. To remedy this, we'll click on **Add media** which will display the media browsing popup dialog which we are already familiar with, and we can choose to upload new images, link images from existing websites, or use the **Library** tab to create an album gallery from images you've already uploaded or linked previously. In the **Library** tab, you can choose multiple images simply by clicking on each of them. When you're done, click on **Submit** and it will add the images to the gallery we've just created (if you are seeing another instance of the Media browser popup window, simply disregard and click on **Cancel**, this is yet again, due to a known bug in this version).

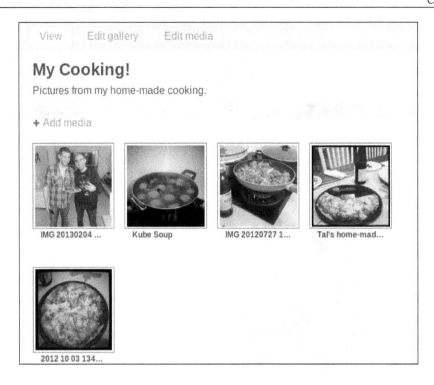

While in the gallery view, you can take actions upon the added images by hovering over one of them:

- Click on the down-arrow with the gear to the right of the image, and choose whether to **Edit** or **Delete** this image.
- Simply drag-and-drop the image to rearrange the pictures order.

When we created the gallery, we set the presentation settings to show media in a lightbox, for which we also installed the Colorbox library. If you click on one of the images in your gallery, you should see it opening up in a popup view, which is often referred to as a lightbox, similar to this one:

In the lightbox view, we can navigate back and forth through images (using the arrow keys too, which is handy), as well as see the image title and description, as we've set in the gallery settings or download the original image. We can also enable the slideshow mode which will automatically load the next image every 3 seconds.

The Image Gallery module, upon installation, created a main menu entry to show all the galleries in your site:

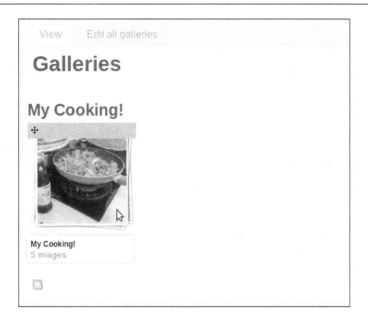

To access this view, navigate to /galleries and you will see the album gallery that we have created just now. Galleries show up with thumbnail of the first media resource in that specific gallery, as well as provide additional information on each gallery when hovering over which displays the title and the type and count of media resources. This galleries view supports the same drag-and-drop behavior which we've seen with images, so by hovering-and-dragging galleries we can rearrange their order. There's even an RSS feed created for all galleries view.

We can further customize the galleries view page by clicking on **Edit all galleries** tab and set the following:

- Title and description text for this page
- The URL for the galleries view, for example change /galleries to /rezepiz-gallery to be SEO-friendly
- The layout of gallery thumbnails and title text placement

Galleries as blocks

Among the usual node settings that we are used to see when adding or editing a node, we can find yet another capability that the Media Gallery module provides—creating blocks for our galleries, which we can then be placed anywhere we'd like, through the use of Drupal's block systems and the available regions the theme defines.

To explore this capability, let's return to the gallery that we've created previously. Locate the **Edit gallery** tab at the top and click on it. We've seen this settings page before, when we first added the gallery. Scroll down and in the **Blocks** field-set, toggle on the option to create a block and feel free to change the default columns and rows as you wish and click on **Save** (usually blocks are placed in thin columns so it's probably best to limit the columns to no more than three).

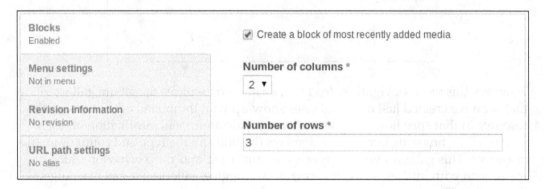

The Media Gallery module has created the block for this gallery but we'll need to use the blocks configuration page to enable it and place it in one of the regions our theme allows.

Navigate to **Structure** | **Blocks** (`/admin/structure/blocks`) and locate a new block named similar to **Recent gallery items: My Cooking!** and should probably be placed in the **Disabled blocks** area at the bottom of the page. We'll add it to the left sidebar regions so in the **REGION** column choose the **Sidebar first** option for this block and click on **Save blocks**. Then locate our galleries block and click on the **configure** link in the rightmost table column labeled **OPERATIONS**. Now we can further customize the block, most important of which is the columns and rows, the block's title and the visibility settings at the bottom (you might want to remove the pages listed there for the sake of this example, so that you will see this block in every page).

When visiting your site's homepage (or other pages), the cooking gallery block will be featuring the latest images and will benefit from the lightbox support too, when clicking on each image.

Summary

In this chapter, we dived into deep water with creating our very own content type for a food recipe website. In order to provide better user experience when dealing with images in Drupal sites, we learned about the prominent Media module and its extensive support for media resources such as providing a media library and key integration with other modules such as the Media Gallery.

With hope of formatting our text inputs better, we have also discovered the concept of text format profiles and the use of WYSIWYG editors to enable a much better experience for content authors.

In the next chapter, we will explore HTML5 specification and how to leverage its features in Drupal to keep our site up-to-date with current technology standards.

4
HTML5 in Drupal

HTML5 transitioned from yet another buzzword that's been circling the web, and a draft spec by the **World Wide Web Consortium (W3C)** http://www.w3c.org, to an implemented set of tools that is truly changing the way we interact with the web.

What were we using before HTML5? Well, that would technically be HTML4, which had released its spec back in 1997, with some revisions later on, and other specs such as XHTML. Since then, we counted on numerous JavaScript libraries and browser plugins, to push browser capabilities to its limits. But all of this is ancient history now since HTML5 has revolutionized the web cyberspace once again.

In this chapter, we will cover:

- Introducing HTML5
- HTML5 spec, features, capabilities
- Using HTML5 in Drupal

Why another HTML spec update? It's just to name a couple of issues that HTML5 targets:

- **Compatibility**: The browser ecosystem is very fragmented, with each vendor implementing only parts of the spec that they see relevant, and still, their implementation has its own quirks across different browsers. To remedy this, the spec strives to detail as much as possible and promote native in-browser support for most features, to avoid third-party plugin dependency.

- **Separate presentation from content**: HTML5 attempts to set a path for semantically structured documents, by providing proper elements to represent content instead of generic placeholders (like the famous <div> tag). With this approach, it hopes to leave presentation task to CSS and has deprecated the elements like <center>, <big>, and <u>, as well as many attributes such as height and width, from specific elements.

HTML5 introduces semantic elements which further help to structure a website using markup. If we used to have the `<div>` elements with different classes or IDs, which defined their purpose earlier, HTML5 provides new elements such as `<section>`, `<article>`, `<header>`, and `<footer>`, now. Frontend developers, those who are associated with developing client-side technologies, which run and render in the user's browser, use the same `<div>` element approach to structure menus and for navigation. HTML5 meets this requirement as well, by introducing elements such as `<nav>` and `<aside>`, just to name a few.

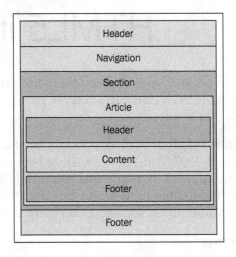

Example of an HTML5 basic page skeleton:

Downloading the example code:

You can download the example code files for all Packt books you have purchased from your account at `http://www.packtpub.com`. If you purchased this book elsewhere, you can visit `http://www.packtpub.com/support` and register to have the files e-mailed directly to you.

```
<!DOCTYPE html>
<html>
  <head>
    <meta charset="utf8">
    <title> Drupal HTML5 Examples </title>
  </head>
  <body>

    <header>
      <h1> Drupal Basic Skeleton HTML5 Page </h1>
    </header>
```

```
<nav>
  <ul>
    <li> <a href="#"> Recipz </a> </li>
    <li> <a href="#"> Memos </a> </li>
  </ul>
</nav>
<section>
  <article>
    <header>
      <h1> Recipe Content Type article </h1>
    </header>
    <p> Recipe content type article text </p>

  </article>
  <footer>
    <p> Read more articles here </p>
  </footer>
</section>

<footer>
  <address>
    email us at test@example.com
  </address>
  <p> Website created by PacktPub's Drupal 7 Media book
    users </p>
</footer>

  </body>
</html>
```

 When opening this in the browser, it will look as plain text, much like a document. This is because we haven't included and made use of any CSS, for styling our HTML code.

It's not all about new HTML elements, but also providing APIs for other features, just to name a few:

- drag and drop, of objects into the browser
- playing music and videos, natively in the browser
- drawing graphics
- real-time communication between browser and server (beyond AJAX), through web socket feature
- offline browser storage, structured and unstructured, beyond cookies
- geolocation
- application caching manifests

It should be noted that HTML5 spec is still considered to be in draft, and there are bits and pieces of it which are being decided upon, on-the-fly, much influenced by how the web is evolving. Moreover, as with all the new things, insecure and improper use of HTML5 properties may lead to security vulnerabilities, which haven't yet been addressed.

 Internet Explorer is likely to get the least score for supporting HTML5 features. IE7 and IE8 are definitely out of scope for HTML5, as they offer very limited support. Latest versions of Opera, Firefox, and Chrome, however, are considered up-to-date with most of HTML5 spec. Some websites like HTML5 test (`http://html5test.com`), offer insight to such information, as well as `http://www.browserscope.org` and `http://caniuse.com`.

HTML5 form elements

You probably remember the times when we turned to JavaScript libraries to implement a horizontal or vertical range bars. How about implementing a widget for the user to input the time, colors, or even email addresses? We've always turned to old faithful JavaScript, but not any more.

With HTML5, we gain semantic elements, such as the following input element examples:

- A form input element for specifying a range:

  ```
  <input type="range" min="0" max="100" value="50" />
  ```

  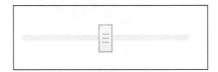

- A form input element for specifying the time:

  ```
  <input type="time" />
  ```

  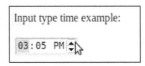

- A form input element for specifying a color:

```
<input type="color" />
```

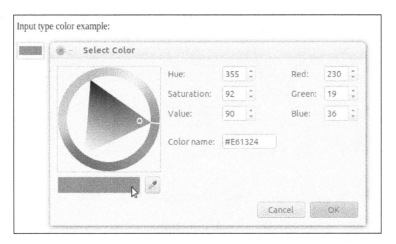

HTML5 media

It was not so long ago that Shockwave Flash technology by Adobe was not supported on the iPhone. This had directly impacted the users—with the inability to surf those websites, which depended on it, to stream content. This, among many other reasons, gave merit to open standards, and the need to have compatibility across the various end user devices such as tablets, smartphones, and desktops, without vendor lock-in.

To understand this better, one needs to realize that music and movies were not as popular as an on-demand service, a few years back. YouTube, which contributed to the rise of video sharing, was founded only at 2005, and showed great potential growth by late 2006.

Browsers were not equipped with the ability to play and manage the streaming of video or audio media. Adding to that, the plethora of file containers and codecs (you know these as divx, xvid, mpeg2, mpeg4, and so on), it's understandable why this was a task that browsers did not take upon themselves. Adobe's Flash technology and Microsoft's Media Server solutions dominated the video and audio streaming capabilities that ruled the web, and as you know, users were mostly dependent on installing the required browser plugins to consume this content.

In the media arena, HTML5 provides the `<video>` and `<audio>` tags, which modern browsers like Opera, Chrome, or Firefox support, and thus provide the capability to simply specify the media resource file, and files will natively play in the browser, without the need for the user to install a plugin in the client side, nor the website builder to install streaming software in the server-side.

Example of using HTML5's `<video>` element:

```
<video
  src="my_movie.ogg"
  poster="my_movie.png"
  controls>
Your browser does not support HTML5's video media
</video>
```

The above code snippet of HTML5 markup specifies the following:

- `src`: The video source file to play, most probably this will always be a resource on a remote server
- `poster`: The picture to display as the thumbnail of the video
- `controls`: Tells the browser to show movie navigation controls like back, forward, and the timeline

Assuming you have provided a sample OGG movie and any PNG or JPG images will do for the poster attribute. Adding the preceding code snippet of the `<video>` tag to our HTML5 basic page skeleton from earlier, you should see something as follows:

Drupal 7 Media - HTML5 Video example

If the browser does not support playing video natively, the contents between the opening and closing `<video>` tags will render, in our example, it will notify the user of their browser's lack of HTML5 support.

Not every media format is supported using these media tags, and it's not just about implementing every possible codec, but rather about promoting those which adhere to good compression quality and low processor cycle demands, which is an even stronger argument when mobile devices come to play. The current draft suggests that browsers should be able to play Theora video, Vorbis audio, and the OGG container format, and it prefers those which are patent-free for best cross-compatibility thus freeing the user from license issues.

Nowadays, the formats used throughout the web are divided due to commercial parties' interests. Google wishes to promote its own WebM format which is open and free too, while Apple and Microsoft gain patent royalties from users of the H264 format. As site builders, you will often find yourself in a need to play well with all browsers, and the video tags make this possible by allowing to specify more than one source file and it's format, which browsers can then choose which out of the listed items they support, and use that as the media source.

Containers versus Codecs

Codec, shorthand for compressor-decompressor, is responsible for compressing data from raw input. This action is usually referred to as encoding. The codec acts to decompress data too, which usually happens when you're viewing a video or listening to an audio file. A container is used to wrap the compressed data and all its metadata. Popular video containers for HTML5 are H264 and OGG, along with their supported codecs: H264, MP4 and Theora. Supported audio containers are H264 and OGG, while their codec's support is: AAC, MP3, and Vorbis.

Example for support fall-back media:

```
<video
  poster="my_movie.png"
  controls>
<source src="my_movie.ogg" type="video/ogg; codecs=
  'theora, vorbis'" />
<source src="my_movie.webm" type="video/webm; codecs=
  vp8.0, vorbis'" />
Your browser does not support HTML5's video media
</video>
```

Another way of dealing with browsers' support for different codecs is to convert video media that has been uploaded to other supported codecs. This requires a lot of consideration, such as infrastructure availability due to CPU-hungry resources that such task requires as well as storage capacity and bandwidth planning. Luckily, if you want to add such capability there are a few Drupal modules that can help with this: `https://drupal.org/project/media_derivatives` and `https://drupal.org/project/video`.

HTML5 canvas

Canvas is a 2D bitmap drawing capability (3D canvas context can be used by **Web Graphics Library (WebGL)**) that browsers provide and expose, JavaScript APIs, to interact with. It's completely integrated into HTML5 documents, controlled using JavaScript, and styled using CSS. As opposed to vector systems like **Scalable Vector Graphics (SVG)**, which is not part of the HTML5 spec, bitmap objects are drawn non-layered, as a flat picture, thus modifying objects, already on the canvas, will affect the entire canvas element.

Uses for canvas technology can vary from providing, in-browser, free-style drawing (think Microsoft Paint in your browser), create games, and create graphs. All of which is natively supported, within the browser, without requiring the use of Flash or other third-party plugins.

Using the canvas feature is possible by simply stating a new element as follows:

```
<canvas height="800" width="600" id="freestyle_draw">
Your browser does not support HTML5 canvas
</canvas>
```

The canvas is only manipulated using JavaScript programming API, which means that just placing the `<canvas>` element, as stated in the preceding code snippet, will not give you a "whiteboard" to draw on, but rather just prepares the ground for later JavaScript work that needs to be done.

When it comes to drawing, you can think of the canvas as a Cartesian coordinates system, where objects that are being drawn upon it, should be specified in respective X and Y coordinates, along with width and height properties.

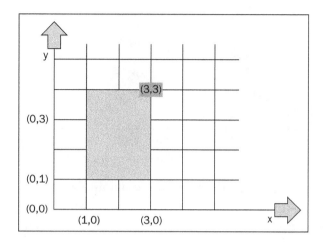

To experiment a little, let's add the following code snippet to our HTML5 basic page skeleton:

```
<script>

//Controlling the canvas using javascript:
var canvasObject = document.getElementById("freestyle_draw");
var canvas = canvasObject.getContext("2d");

//Define the canvas background
canvas.fillStyle = "rgb(255, 0, 0)";
//Define the drawing color
canvas.strokeStyle = "rgb(255, 255, 255)";

//Draw a rectangle somewhere at the top
//fillRect(x, y, w, h)
canvas.fillRect(50, 50, 100, 100)

</script>
```

This should produce a result as follows:

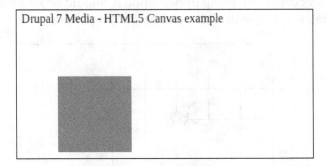

More ideas for what could be done with the canvas feature:

- Embedding images into the canvas, and manipulating them.

- Moving objects, because we can create and control everything in the canvas using JavaScript API. We can animate graphics; this is how movies and games are made.

- Canvas brings in new possibilities for web applications. To meet these new standards, and provide tools to leverage such HTML5 features, game, and drawing engines are being developed to accommodate this evolving future.

HTML5 resources

There are many resources on the web where one can find information about HTML5; specifically, we chose to note the following:

- `http://html5doctor.com`: A website and a blog, which aims to educate and promote HTML5 spec through articles hosting HTML5 elements resource information

- `http://caniuse.com`: A website that provides information about desktop and mobile browsers capabilities, around HTML5

- `http://www.html5rocks.com`: A website and blog that is run by HTML5 advocates and web developers, who work at companies like Google, deusingntART, Adobe, Incapsula, and others, who aim to promote HTML5 through articles, tutorials, and other online resources

For those who wish to boost their HTML5 knowledge through the means of professional and focused books, you can find the following books by Packt Publishing, among many others:

- HTML5 Canvas Cookbook (`http://www.packtpub.com/html5-canvas-cookbook-recipes-to-revolutionize-web-experience/book`)

- HTML5 Multimedia Development (`http://www.packtpub.com/html5-multimedia-development-cookbook/book`)

- HTML5 Web Application Development by example (`http://www.packtpub.com/html5-web-application-development-using-css3-jquery/book`)

HTML5 in Drupal

With the growth of HTML5, modules are beginning to ramp up. They utilize HTML5 features like support for a geolocation field, video and audio media elements, and online drawing, through the canvas. It's not all about modules, but also themes are already available to provide up-to-date support with HTML5 standards such as responsive design through the use of media queries, structuring the HTML page itself, and much more.

We'll examine a Drupal module, which adds support for some of the HTML5 fields that we covered (it introduces other HTML5 capabilities, but we can focus on the fields for now). The module is called **HTML5 Tools** and we'll download and install Version 7.x-1.2 (`http://drupal.org/project/html5_tools`), but notice that it depends on the module (7.x-1.3) too, which we'll need to download and install as well (`http://drupal.org/project/elements`) for HTML5 Tools to work.

After installing both modules we will proceed to add some HTML5 fields to the
rezepi content type that we've already created. Navigate to **Structure | Content
Types | rezepi | manage fields** (`/admin/structure/types/manage/rezepi/
fields`), and we'll begin by adding a range field for users to be able to specify the
amount of cooking time. In the **Add new field** row, we'll call the new field **Cooking
Time**, set the **FIELD TYPE** option to **Integer**, and choose **Range Field** for the
WIDGET column. Click on **Save**, in the field settings set **Minimum** to `1`, **Maximum**
to `180`, **Prefix** to `1`, **Suffix** to `180 minutes`, and click on **Save settings**. We've now
created a range field with allowed values of 1 to 180, and set the prefix and suffix
text to be used when the widget draws, so that the actual range that is being used,
is clear to the user.

Minimum

```
1
```

The minimum value that should be allowed in this field. Leave blank for no minimum.

Maximum

```
180
```

The maximum value that should be allowed in this field. Leave blank for no maximum.

Prefix

```
1
```

Define a string that should be prefixed to the value, like '$ ' or '€ '. Leave blank for none. Separate singular and plural values
with a pipe ('pound|pounds').

Suffix

```
180 minutes
```

Define a string that should be suffixed to the value, like ' m', ' kb/s'. Leave blank for none. Separate singular and plural values
with a pipe ('pound|pounds').

For the sake of an example, we'll add a number field to be used for the oven temperature degrees. In the content type's configuration page add a new field **Cooking Temperature**, choose the **Integer** option as **FIELD TYPE** again, and now set the **WIDGET** column to **Number field**, and click on **Save**. We can set the field settings as, **Minimum** to 1, **Maximum** to 300, which guides the user regarding the range of values to be typed in.

HTML5 Tools module provides other fields too. If you look closely on the **Text** field type, you can see that we now have some new options such as **Email field**, **URL field**, and **Telephone number field**. If you're wondering what's the point of a telephone field then think of mobile devices, if they detect a telephone field type then the keyboard that will pop up on the mobile device will be all digits. It's more convenient to the user, and also less error-prone.

Let's add a new **rezepi** content type and see the new fields in action:

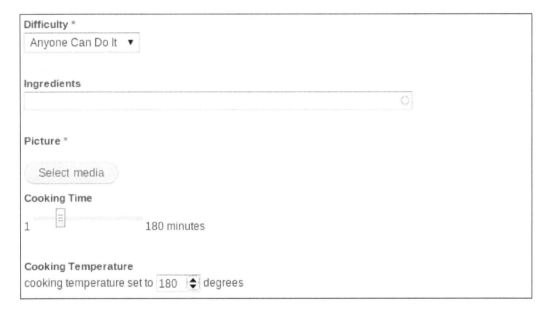

Like we mentioned earlier, HTML5 Tools comes with more options to make your Drupal site HTML5-ready than just form fields. These options can be configured in **Configuration | Development | HTML5 Tools** (`/admin/config/development/html5-tools`), and they feature a settings which hook into the page layout and modify how the HTML page is structured. Some of these options modify the `<html>` tag, others just clean out the `<script>` tags:

OVERRIDE DRUPAL'S FORMS WITH THEIR HTML5 COUNTERPARTS

☑ Site information

Modify the site configuration email textfield to an email field.

☑ Search block

Modify the search block textfield to a search field.

☑ Search form

Modify the search form textfield to a search field.

☑ User registration

Modify the user registration textfield to an email field.

☑ Contact forms

Modify contact form's textfields to email fields.

SIMPLIFY <HEAD> MARKUP

☑ Simplify doctype

Replaces html.tpl.php with a custom html.tpl.php which has the proper html5 doctype. This settings will not take effect if your theme has its own html.tpl.php.

☑ Simplify style tags

Removes the type attribute from links to stylesheets. The format for HTML5 is *<link rel="stylesheet" href="file.css" />*. The *type="text/css"* is unnecessary.

☑ Simplify javascript tags

Removes the type attribute from the <script> tag. The format for HTML5 is *<script src="file.js"></script>*. The *type="text/javascript"* is unnecessary. All browsers will assume it is javascript.

☑ Simplify meta tags

Alters the *http-equiv="content-type"* meta tag to make it shorter, removing the http-equiv and content attributes. They are unnecessary.

☑ Add Google Chrome Frame headers

Adds the X-UA-Compatible: IE=Edge,chrome=1 headers for IE browsers. This will not prompt the user to install Google Chrome Frame, it'll just use it if available.

For the rest of the book it might be best if you disable HTML5 Tools module as it may conflict with the theme we have already enabled, which supports HTML5 standards, so at the very least, there's no need for both of them installed with their default configuration settings.

A canvas playground

If you ever wanted to add a feature for drawing in your site, or even possibly, create a web application all around the ability to simply draw, then we're going to explore this functionality.

Some ideas for web applications related to drawing:

- Provide a mechanism to digitally sign on everything. With the rise of mobile and tablets adoption, now more than ever, what used to be just a website operated by a mouse and keyboard to navigate, are now getting the stylus and fingertips, dimension which spices up things.

- Provide the ability to simply draw. That sounds too ordinary for you? Something that is too easy? Well, the mobile app Draw Something, will disagree, and it has popularity and download statistics, to back it up. Just spice up your web application with some gamification, social networking sharing, and you're probably on your way to forming a cool web application.

After we've established that, there are at least some use cases for using an in-browser drawing capability, let's start leveraging that to our own needs, starting with installing a module that should do the job: **Canvas field**.

As always, we'll need to download the Canvas field module (`http://drupal.org/project/canvas_field`), and install it. At the time of writing this book, there's only a development version available (7.x-1.x-dev) so we'll use that. Download, unpack, and enable this module, either manually, using Drush, or by using Drupal 7's GUI for installing modules.

Creating a content type for the canvas field

Our plan is to go with the signature idea, enabling users to supply their signatures when creating content. The use case will be as follows: a user uploads a document, like an NDA (Non-disclosure agreement), for example, which require other parties to provide their signatures after they reviewed the document.

The Canvas field ties into this requirement very closely because under the hood it introduces a new Drupal field type, which we can add to a new node content type that we will create.

Based on the above, we will name our new node content type **DigiDoc** because it sounds cool, and fits well with our description of the use case. Aside from the usual title and description fields, it will need to have a file upload field to store the actual documents, and then an unlimited amount of Canvas field instances, so that we can collect more than one signature.

We won't cover the step by step actions required to create this content type as you are probably familiar with this process by now (you could quickly read through *Chapter 1, Drupal's Building Blocks* to remind yourself of how we went about doing this). A quick look into our almost ready **DigiDoc** content type, which lacks the canvas field (we will focus on that in a minute), is as follows:

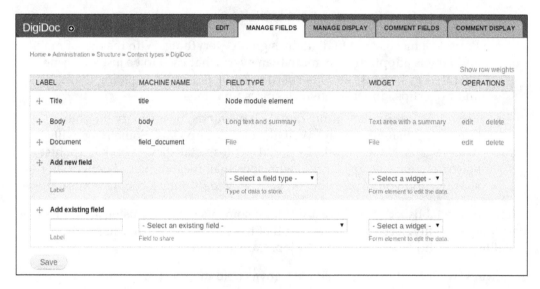

Our next field will be named **Signatures** and it will use the **Image** field type, and for the widget we'll use the newly provided option, **Canvas Widget**, and click on **Save**.

You may now see the initial and short, **FIELD SETTINGS** page, continue with that by clicking on **Save field settings**, which will bring us to the field settings page to update all of the settings.

Except for the default settings that we know, such as setting a **Help text** field for this field (which in our case is probably something you should know, to make it obvious to the user), or toggling the **Required field** option to on or off, the canvas field module added a few more settings here, first of which are the **STYLE** settings which determine the canvas size, colors, and overall layout. It's probably good to choose a canvas size that is small, and fits a rectangle shape that resembles a signature field that you see in documents.

 The latest version of the canvas module has a bug where the color settings it accepts for **Background Color** and **Border Color**, must be prefixed with the hash (#) tag, and not as stated in the example, yet the input text is limited to 6 characters only. The workaround is to specify the hex color code using the shorthand notation using only three characters, including the hash tag, that's four, and it will work ok. A bug on this has already been opened, and a patch exists in the issue queue.

We'll also toggle on the **Allow Color Selection** checkbox to spice up the signatures. This can actually open up a cool feature in your web application where the users that sign get a unique color each .Next set of options that the canvas field module provides, allow to define the behavior of the canvas field when adding or editing content. With the default settings, when adding a new DigiDoc content the canvas field will actually render as a drawable canvas, while when editing an existing DigiDoc content the canvas field will render as an image that would not allow for editing the already-drawn canvas picture. The defaults are ok for now so we will continue with the suggested behavior, where a signed picture turns into a file download and is not editable after submitted.

Lastly, to meet our use case of allowing more than one party to sign the document we will need to set the **Number of values** field at the bottom of the screen to **Unlimited**, and then click on **Save settings**.

Creating a new DigiDoc

Now we're ready to start using our new **DigiDoc** content type.

To add a new DigiDoc navigate to the **Add content** page (/node/add) and click on the **DigiDoc** content type to proceed with creating it.

Set the **Title** and **Body** fields with some text for our new DigiDoc:

Next field is the file upload **Document** field, which as you can see I've set it as a required field when configuring this content type, as well as configured some common file extensions for the **Allowed file types** setting:

And finally, the canvas field module lives up to the promise of providing in-browser drawing capability:

A couple of things you can notice straight away about the canvas drawing board:

- It is set to the height and width that we configured when creating the **DigiDoc** content type

- It includes basic drawing tools like the pencil, a button to clear out the canvas completely, and buttons for changing the background and foreground colors (which we also enabled and configured earlier)

I bet you are goofing around now with the drawing board! And to think you thought, what's the fun in that, just a short while ago. So take your time to work on that vice-president signature of yours, and when you're done, instead of submitting the form we'll click on **Add another** button to see how easy it is to manage these signatures.

After clicking on the **Add another** button, our drawing was saved as a PNG picture and uploaded to our website, and it's been added to the **SIGNATURES** listing, which features a thumbnail of the picture that shows our signature in a smaller form scale, and options to **Remove** or **Edit** it.

Assuming we want to change the signature we've just saved, let's click on the **Edit** button:

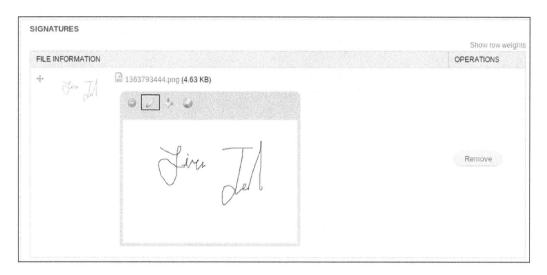

The **Edit** button renders the picture right there in the **SIGNATURES** listing, and allows you to make changes. You can notice that while the drawing toolbar is quite thin on features, it's just a matter of extending it if we choose to. Moreover, now when you're actually doing the drawing, you can notice the big difference between Canvas and SVG, where Canvas is just a flat drawing board, as opposed to SVG which is layered and you can make discrete changes to objects on the drawing board.

Once we're done playing around with the signatures, let's click on the **Save** button, and see how it looks like in the full node view:

View   Edit

NDA of our new startup - digidoc

Submitted by lirantal on Wed, 03/20/2013 - 17:47

Please read carefully through the attached document and provide signatures by editing this digidoc, adding your own and saving it.

Document:
DigiDoc-Venture-NDA_draft2.docx
Signatures:

Summary

In this chapter, we learned about HTML5 spec, why the web needed it and how to make use of the spec to create, cross-browser, compliant HTML code in Drupal. We furthermore dived into the canvas feature of HTML5, which enable browsers to render picture drawing support with no additional third-party components. With this knowledge, we have even created our very own signature management web application.

In the next chapter, we will look at video support and management in Drupal, and adopt other HTML5 spec features to aid in providing consistent video playing support across browsers.

5
Video Capabilities

In the previous chapters we've talked much about images, and using them in various ways—from embedding them in WYSIWYG editors used by content authors, to creating image galleries. Let's start exploring the use of videos as well, in all of its aspects.

In this chapter, we will cover:

- Adding videos to your site
- Using videos which are both locally hosted on your personal Drupal site as well as hosted on remote services such as YouTube
- Creating video galleries and playlists

With the rise of storage solutions and available capacities, in addition to the increased bandwidth in every house-hold, the popularity of on-demand rich-content media, such as videos, was a sure thing to come. Whether it's video on-demand solutions to stream TV broadcasting, or Internet websites such as YouTube which contributed to this evolution, it is definitely more than a mere trend. To put this in perspective, YouTube started with 100,000,000 daily video views in 2006 and saw growth to a massive 4 billion daily video views by 2012.

The ability for every house-hold to enjoy high-resolution video content is not confined only to the movies industry but it is also changing education. Nowadays one can freely and easily attend MIT's or Stanford University's classes through the web by simply accessing their recorded class sessions through their websites.

Adding videos hosted on third-party websites

In most cases, if your website is not about hosting video content there is almost no need to enable users to upload videos to your website. Instead, you would rather be more interested in providing the best interoperability as possible with other third-party websites such as YouTube, so that your users can share video content from such popular websites.

In this section we will explore how it is made possible to integrate with other websites.

Creating our video content type

Most commonly, users will want to link, embed, or include in some way, videos that have already been made available through third-party websites, such as YouTube, Vimeo, and Metacafe.

Our use case will be to create video content around the music industry, such as sharing videos of favorite bands. Some ideas on how you can take this concept forward and develop it further are as follows:

- By adding social features such as rating, thumbs-up, and some gamification where you can create a sort of band-battle where two bands's video-clips are placed one besides the other and users can vote which is better.

- With the surplus of cover song videos on YouTube, maybe it requires its own niche website? Create a website dedicated for cover songs by artists.

- Create a social networking website where bands form the main entity and give them tools to manage their band, tour dates, band members personal blogs, fan club communication and, so much more can be added.

We have previously introduced the use of the Media module and its companion Media Gallery which helped us create and manage image-based content. These basic modules will continue to serve us for the video content as well as other media content in following chapters.

Building on the Media module, we require integration with additional modules to bring support for embedding content from third-party websites. With YouTube being a popular resource for video media we'll make use of the module that provides this integration. We'll start off by downloading and enabling the Media: YouTube module (`http://drupal.org/project/media_youtube`).

The Media module strives to provide APIs for modules to integrate with, using its Media Internet Sources module bindings, to enrich its media functionality. The Media: YouTube module is one of those but it's not the only one. There are dozens of other modules available on drupal.org to provide this integration that you might be looking for, some of which are TED, Flickr, Facebook, and Vimeo, just to name a few.

To share a band's music videos we'll create a new node content type called Vidz which aside from the usual title and description field will also have a field to include videos. Go to **Structure | Content Types | + Add content type** (admin/structure/types/add) and after naming this new content type Vidz (you may choose your own cool name for it too) and click on **Save and add fields** which will take us straight to the **MANAGE FIELDS** tab for this content type so that we can get to work.

We'll call our new field Video (it's generic enough to accommodate future changes too to our site's purpose) and choose the **Multimedia asset** field type along with the only widget available for that right now, which is **Media file selector** as shown in the following screenshot:

After clicking on the **Save** button we're headed over to the general field settings page, as usual we'll continue forward by clicking on **Save field settings** to edit the actual field's settings.

We'll need to configure the field settings for enabling video content from YouTube for our users, first of which is the **Enabled browser plugins** as shown in the following screenshot:

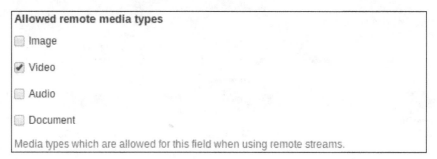

There's no interest for now to allow users to upload video files but only to link them through sites such as YouTube, which is the only integration bridge we enabled at this point. So the only options you should toggle on for this setting is the **Web** and **YouTube** browsing options, when the media browser pop-up dialog shows up.

Next we will allow specifying only video content type links so **Video** is the only option that is toggled on as shown in the following screenshot:

For the **Allowed URI schemes** setting we'll toggle off the **public://** option so that users would not be able to link to videos that have been uploaded somehow to our local Drupal site (at least, we're not interested in that for the time being) as shown in the following screenshot:

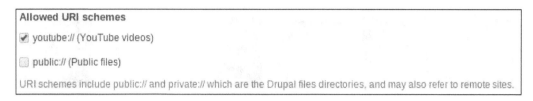

Leaving the default setting for **Number of values** field of 1, we're now done, so click on the **Save settings** button and let's navigate to creating a new Vidz entry via **Add content | Vidz** (/node/add/vidz).

Adding a new video using the YouTube browser

In the **Create Vidz** page, scroll down to the **Video** field and click on **Select media** to review our media browser options as shown in the following screenshot:

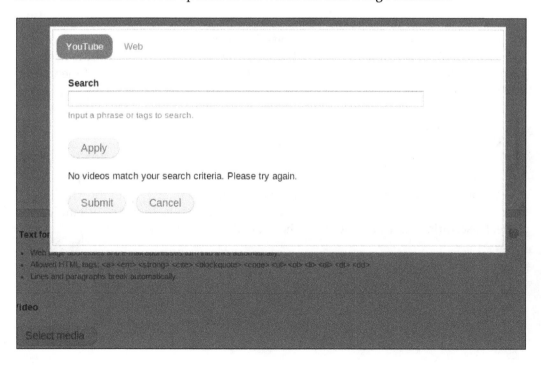

Because we enabled the YouTube browsing options when we configured the **Video** field earlier, it's now available for us and provides very basic browsing through YouTube videos right there in the tab. Type-in a search text and click on **Apply**, let's see how results render as shown in the following screenshot:

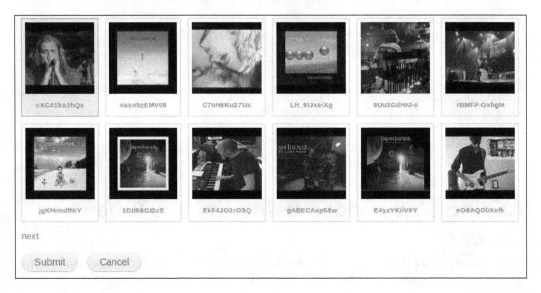

I've typed in `dream theater`, one of my favorite bands and always a good choice for me as background music when I write code. Because we've enabled only one value to be chosen it's impossible to multi-select a couple of videos. If you want to keep navigating the search results click on the **next** link, otherwise select one of the videos and click on **Submit**.

 If you're wondering what are those random characters beneath every video then these are the video ids as they are saved by YouTube, unique for each video.

As you probably remember from previously working on images with the Media module, it provides further addition of fields to media assets, in our case it added **Title**, **Description**, and **Tags** fields as shown in the following screenshot:

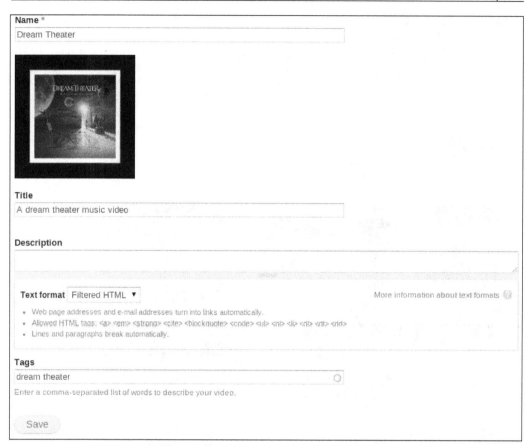

Once we have filled in all the details and clicked on **Save** for the selected video we can see that the Media module also took care of grabbing a thumbnail for the video which makes a nice addition when this gets displayed later on in various display modes as shown in the following screenshot:

And finally, when viewing our Vidz content in full view display mode, the video we chose renders into YouTube's embedded player, including a thumbnail preview. Clicking on the player's play button will start streaming the video straight from your Drupal site as shown in the following screenshot:

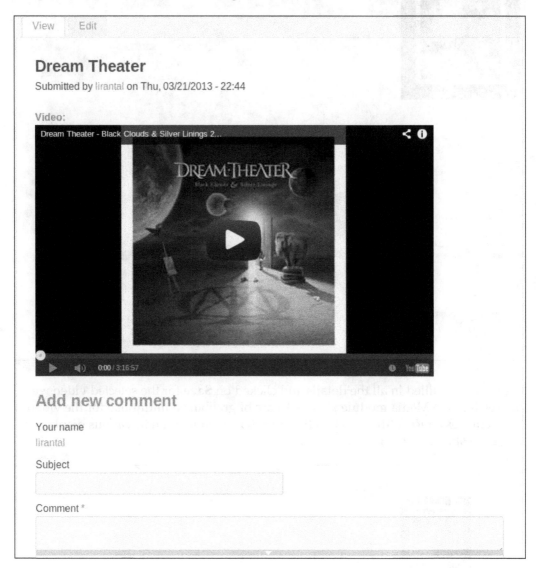

Adding a new video using URL

While browsing through the YouTube browser option for adding videos seems like a nice feature, and it is, it's still not functional enough for users to really make use of it. For example, you can't play the selected video from the browsing pop-up dialog box. Picking and choosing the video you need, unless you know exactly which video you're looking for just by the thumbnail, this will be rather hard.

For this reason, most chances are that you've got a YouTube link for a video, or simply the video itself opened in another browser tab or window. From that point, the easiest thing to do is simply to copy and paste the URL. Let's see how that is done.

Create a new Vidz content type or simply edit the one we had just created (I chose the latter as it's simpler). Clicking now on the **Select media** button and choosing the **Web** tab in the popup dialog we can specify the URL for the video, just as it shows up in our browser's address bar when viewing the video from YouTube's website as shown in the following screenshot:

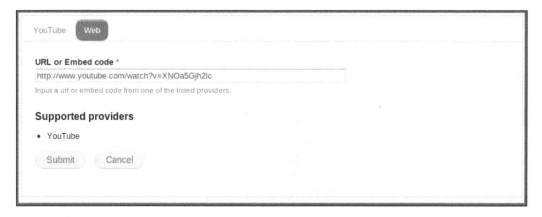

Notice how the **Web** tab also lists the allowed providers, from which you can copy and paste a URL. Using YouTube is possible because we installed the integration module for it. If we wanted to support more third-party video providers, we can do it by installing their related modules and all of them will be listed to notify the user which providers are supported.

After clicking on **Submit** we see the same video settings form which sets all the fields, although notice how when using the URL copy and paste option the video name was already retrieved for us:

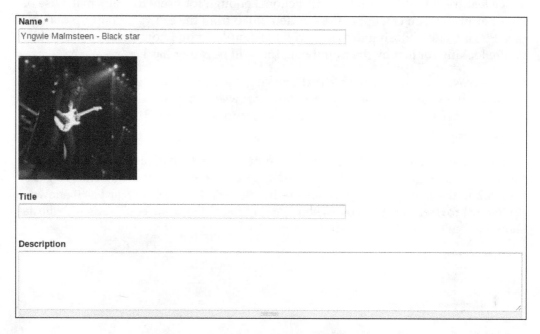

Embedding videos in WYSIWYG editor

It might be desired for content authors to embed videos using the WYSIWYG editor and placing these media resources and styling them in their own way, around their text. Because we have previously enabled the Media Browser functionality and integrated it with our CKEditor WYSIWYG editor we gain this functionality now with zero effort.

Create or edit an existing Vidz content type entry and switch the **Body** field to use the **Full HTML** option for the **Text format** field. Now the plain text area input field should have rendered into a rich text editor and the Media Browser button is available. Clicking on it, will open the Media Browser and allow you to add YouTube media as we've done before with the dedicated video field, so we won't be going over this procedure again as shown in the following screenshot:

You may have noticed that the Media Browser popup dialog shows all available options to add media, whether it's the **YouTube** and **Web** tabs that we've just been using or the other options like **Upload** and **Library** tabs which we've seen when creating images before.

You may be wondering why this happens because when we configured the video field for the Vidz content type we strictly defined which Media Browser options to display. The answer is that this happens because the Media Browser WYSIWYG editor button is de-coupled from the fields that are assigned to the content type or their configuration. The configuration for the Media Browser WYSIWYG editor button happens in a site-global configuration option at **Configuration | Media | Media browser settings** (/admin/config/media/browser) which probably looks as follows:

As you can see, the **Enabled browser plugins** options are all toggled off, which means that all of them will be showing up. If we had wanted to only display the **Web** and **YouTube** tabs on the Media Browser dialog then we need to select them (and possibly also remove the **Image** and **Audio** options from the **Allowed types in WYSIWYG** field). Consider carefully if this is the desired configuration for your site because these settings apply site-wide to all content types that the Media Browser WYSIWYG button appears for.

Customizing videos

Being able to add videos to your Drupal site is nice and it really opens up lots of possibilities but this functionality out of the box may not be enough at times.

You may often find yourself required to extend videos with your own custom fields that suit your content type target audience, or if you're using a third-party videos provider you may want to customize the look and feel of the embedded player for that provider.

Customizing video fields

Due to the Media module providing us with file-type specific configuration, we can take advantage of that, and configure each file type's behavior and setup. Between extending its fields, to managing its display mode, we gain pretty much complete control over how these media resources are handled.

The fact that the video field we created is actually a File entity, allows us to extend it with our own fields that will attach to the video that the user provided. In our case, we'd like to extend the default **Title**, **Description**, **Tags**, and **License settings for this audio** fields for a Video file type with some of our own which are relevant to music videos.

Targeting for music videos, there are some obvious fields for us to add, such as the year it was recorded, whether it was recorded at a studio or a live performance, the music composer(s) and the lyricist(s).

To manage the Video file type fields we'll navigate to **Structure | File Types | Video | manage fields** (`/admin/structure/file-types/manage/video/fields`) as shown the in the following screenshot:

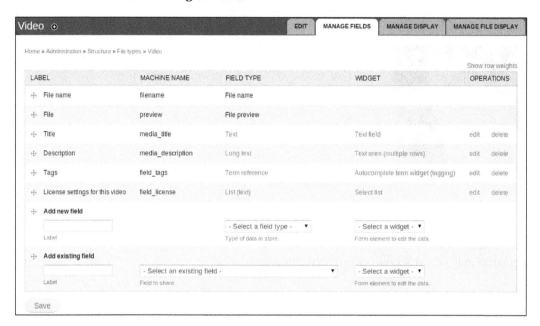

We'll add our own fields, as mentioned previously and the final fields configuration is as follows:

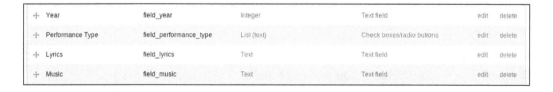

When adding a new YouTube video now, the fields settings options which show up before we save the video would be as shown in the following screenshot:

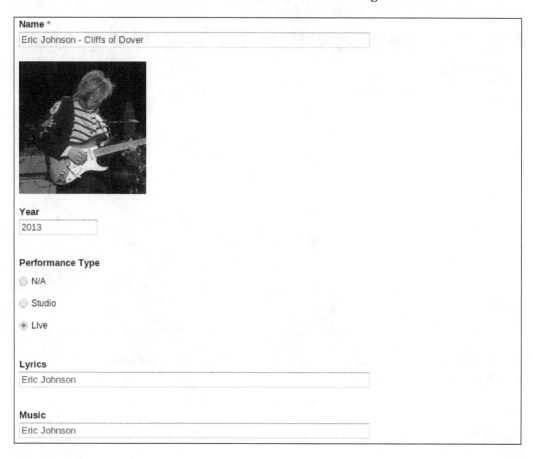

Some ideas for more fields if you wish to build on this are as follows:

- **Band members**: A field with a list of band members in each music video, you can then link to their user profile page on your site, and users can rate them, leave comments on their wall. Each band member can have a history of the bands he was on, tours, and so on.

- **Rig**: Bands can include the rigs their using, whether it's drums, keyboards, amps, guitars, guitar pedals, and so on. This will probably attract interest for more discussion around each of them and it may even pave the possibility for a business model around sponsored ads for each manufacturer.

- **Location**: By adding a location field you can then provide suggestions to upcoming shows or history of shows and bands in that location. Show these items on a Google Maps layer (yes, there's a Drupal module for that too), add some location-specific analytics and this begins to take on a really cool form.

Customizing video display modes

While the full node view of our Vidz content type shows the embedded YouTube video, this may not be the case for all display modes. If you were hoping to create views later on for this content type or even just simply take a look at your site's home page you would have noticed that there's no trace of media attached to this content:

Dream Theater

Submitted by lirantal on Thu, 03/21/2013 - 22:44

Read more Add new comment

NDA of our new startup - digidoc

Submitted by lirantal on Wed, 03/20/2013 - 17:47

Please read carefully through the attached document and provide signatures by editing this digidoc, adding your own and saving it.

Read more Add new comment

Kubbeh Soup

Submitted by lirantal on Fri, 03/01/2013 - 20:04

This is what we will be making. It looks so yummy!

To solve this, we'll need to make some modifications by heading over to the Vidz content type display settings at **Structure** | **Content Types** | **Vidz** | **manage display** | **Teaser** (`/admin/structure/types/manage/vidz/display/teaser`) where you can see the Video field is actually hidden. To fix this, we'll drag-and-drop the **Video** field below the **Body** field using the arrows icon to the right of the row. At this point we can also hide the **Video** label as it's really not contributing anything if the video is already showing up there. Once you're done click on **Save**, and your configuration for the teaser display mode should look like the following screenshot:

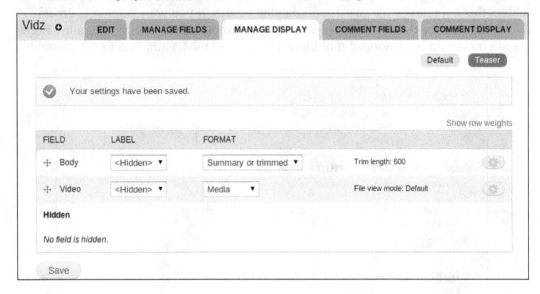

Because we chose the **Default** file view mode, if you go to your site's home page you'll see that the video shows in full, including all the **Video** fields we added earlier (Year, Performance Type, and so on). Not exactly what we hoped for, possibly a bit too much information for a content's teaser view. To fix that we'll go back to the **manage display** page we were on and click on the gear icon to the right of the **Video** column and choose one of the available options:

- **Default**: It shows a full width of the video as you'd see it if you clicked on it, including all of the configured **Video** fields.
- **Teaser**: It shows the video in a slightly smaller size, and allows playing it from the view listing without requiring to see the full node view. It will not list any fields attached to the content.
- **Preview**: It shows a thumbnail of the video, no attached fields, and no ability to play it from that view either.

If you installed the lightbox library from earlier chapters then you'd probably see a bunch of display options that it provides too.

It would probably be best to either choose the **Teaser** or **Preview** mode from the file view mode options, remember to click on the **Save** button after you select one of the options to save the display mode settings.

Customizing YouTube player

If we had wanted to further customize the display mode options it can be done pretty simply. Let's modify the **Preview** file view mode with our set of fields and further even customize the YouTube player settings.

Navigate to **Structure** | **File Types** | **Video** | **manage display** | **Teaser** (/admin/ structure/file-types/manage/video/display/teaser) and drag-and-drop the **Year** and **Performance Type** fields below the **File** field and change their **Label** column setting to **<Inline>**. For the sake of simplicity, we chose an integer field type to represent the year but in practice it would have made a better choice to use a date field module (one that is based on HTML5 too makes an even better choice). Because of this, the formatter for the **Year** field display is probably one of space, decimal point, or comma, as a thousand marker but we're not really interested in any of these for this case so we'll click on that gear icon to configure it and set this option to **<none>** and click on **Update**, followed by **Save** as shown in the following screenshot:

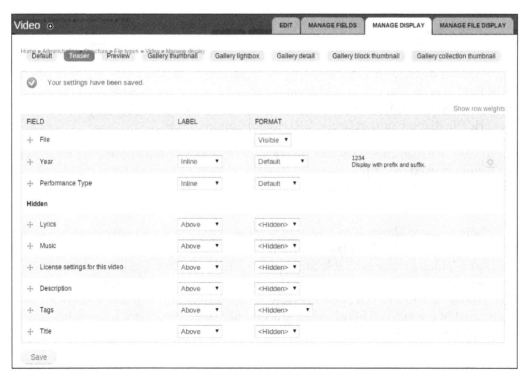

We'll next jump to the **MANAGE FILE DISPLAY** tab (`/admin/structure/file-types/manage/video/file-display`) and click on the **Teaser** tab inside the page to configure the teaser view mode for video type fields. Let's figure out what this configuration is all about:

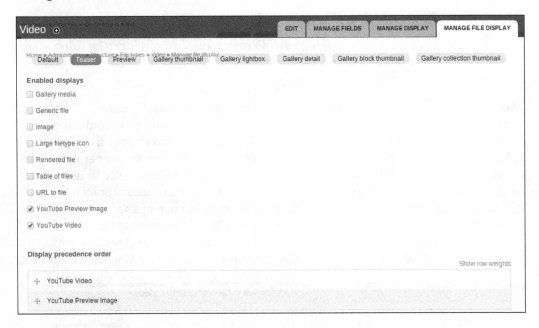

The **Enabled displays** lists the available options to format the file view. For example, if the field was an image it would have made sense to use the **Image** display option or, if you had wanted to simply place a link to the file you could have used the **Generic file** display or maybe the **URL to file** option.

In our case, the **YouTube Preview Image** and **YouTube Video** options are set, where the former is used to simply display a thumbnail view of the YouTube video and the latter is the actual display formatter that renders the YouTube video into an actual playable content.

Why both of them are enabled you may wonder. The idea is that we can set a fallback logic using the **Display precedence order** setting, which shows that if the **YouTube Video** field is available and working, then use that, but if that module may be disabled, or some error that causes this display format to not render the content then it falls back to the **YouTube Preview Image** format and will just display a thumbnail of the video. This allows a graceful fallback mechanism when rendering the display formatters.

The second part of this configuration page provides the display formatter-specific configuration, that is, **Display settings**. Starting with the **YouTube Preview Image** field, we're able to select which **Image style** to use. We've visited this configuration previously when we worked with images, and this setting basically allows you to define the image style (at /admin/config/media/image-styles) which commonly defines the dimensions an image will be scaled to and possibly apply some other image effects too as shown in the following screenshot:

Next in the vertical tab options is the **YouTube Video** display settings. There, we can really fine tune how YouTube's embedded player behaves and looks like.

Beginning with the width and height settings, we can tune the teaser option to a smaller dimension, like that of a thumbnail image for example. Basic theming functionality allows us to define the overall theme color of the player – black or white and progress bar color and functional buttons during playback. More options that the Media: YouTube module provides allow to further tune the player's settings yet they're pretty self-explanatory so we won't dwell on covering each of them (except possibly the last JavaScript API related option which enables programmers to interface with YouTube for further fine-grained control over the video player's behavior as shown in the following screenshot:

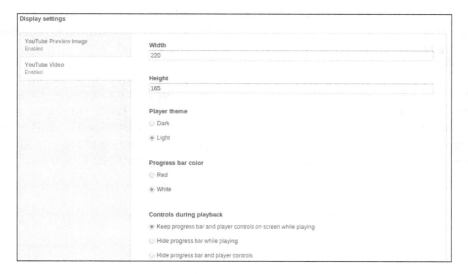

Once we save these settings, let's visit our site's front page and see how our changes affect the content type's listing look, specifically for the Vidz content type:

Adding videos hosted locally

Having good integration facilities with third-party sites around your niche content, and sharing capabilities are pretty basic features you will find in most apps today. You may still want or even need to provide your users with the ability to upload their media content to your site directly.

Uploading video files to your site means that the media is right there in your website to play, but how will you play it? Pre-HTML5 era browsers had to rely on third-party plugins such as QuickTime to play Apple's MOV format, or Adobe's Shockwave Flash format to play the popular SWF format. Due to the fact that movies are naturally not encoded in any of these formats but rather using popular codecs such as DIVX, XVID, MPEG2, or MPEG4, it required to transcode videos from their original format to SWF to be playable over the web, which then introduced demand for more resources (transcoding is a CPU-intensive task).

If all that sounds a bit scary and complex, do not worry, because HTML5 is here now! It pushed browser vendors to provide built-in support for agreed-upon video formats. With this video playing support, browsers provide JavaScript-based API to interact with the media in play. As with everything around open source and open standards, this spawned a myriad of JavaScript libraries wanting to tap into this and feature players that can be skinned, tweaked, and customized in many ways.

Not blind to this, Drupal's modules eco-system soon enough offered relevant solutions, probably most popular are the MediaFront and MediaElement modules, which offer HTML5 video playing, and even feature fallback for Flash capabilities for browsers which lack proper HTML5 support.

 By providing HTML5 media players in your site you're giving guarantee that mobile devices like smartphones and tablets are mostly supported too.

Installing an HTML5 media player

It's a tough choice between media players, each with its own strength. The MediaElement module has better integration with the Media Gallery module so we can seamlessly create galleries, even mixed kinds with pictures and videos, but it isn't as advanced as MediaFront which is packed with advanced theming administration support out of the box, support for playlists and many more.

We'll be using Drupal's MediaElement module which is a light-weight HTML5 video and audio player, based on the `MediaElement.js` library (`http://www.mediaelementjs.com`) and out of the box provides great customizing capabilities, support for playing both video and audio, and fallback for Flash. All of which, makes it a pretty decent selection as our media player.

Because the MediaElement's Drupal module depends on the actual `MediaElement.js` JavaScript library we'll need to get that, so we're better of starting with that one. Surf over to `http://www.mediaelementjs.com` and download the latest edition (at the time of writing the book this was 2.11.0) and place it in the `sites/all/libraries/` directory. If it downloaded as a `master` filename, that's ok, simply unzip it however it is named and rename the directory it unpacked to (probably something like `johndyer-mediaelement-3ee7a7d`) to `mediaelement`. End result is that the `MediaElement.js` file should exist in this path `sites/all/libraries/mediaelement/build/mediaelement.js`.

Download the MediaElement's module (`http://drupal.org/project/mediaelement`), unpack, and enable the module as always, via your favorite method of installation. The module depends on the Libraries API module as well, (`http://drupal.org/project/libraries`) so download it too and enable both of them.

At this point, we're ready to test that everything has been installed correctly. Navigate to MediaElement's module configuration page at **Configuration | Media | MediaElement.js** and you should see a playable video. If you see it and it plays well then everything has been installed correctly and if you inspect that page a little closer you can see that it's playing an MP4 file that's located on your site and has been included in the `MediaElement.js` library when you downloaded it as shown in the following screenshot:

The only real configuration item that the MediaElement module provides is whether or not to include the `MediaElement.js` library in every page load, which is probably not required, unless you're really using it with your own custom code/modules.

Uploading videos and playing them

Even after installing the required modules, if we were to actually upload a video to our Vidz content type, even if this may have been possible to do, we did not configure a file display format to render the uploaded file with an actual media player and it would just render out as a link to the file.

First we need to edit our content type and enable file uploads. Navigate to **Structure | Content Types | Vidz | manage fields** and click on **edit** on the **Video** field row (`/admin/structure/types/manage/vidz/fields/field_video`).

Because we have previously only worked on having video files play from third-party hosting providers using their APIs, we did not yet enable the option to upload files to our Drupal site. To fix that, let's change the **Allowed file extensions for uploaded files** field to include video formats and also the **Enabled browser plugins** so that we can have the **Upload** and the **Library** tabs in addition to embedding files from external sites such YouTube as shown in the following screenshot:

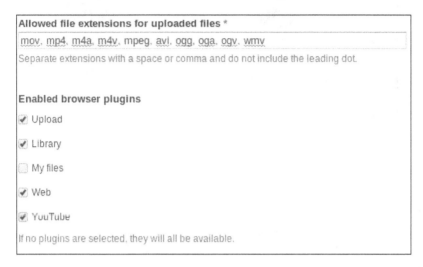

In the same page, we'll also allow the **public://** scheme which means we can reference files located in our local Drupal install:

Now it's time to tell Drupal how to render video files which are hosted locally. Navigate to **Structure | File Types | Video | manage file display** and for the **Default** file display mode we'll also toggle on the **MediaElement Video** display option as shown in the following screenshot:

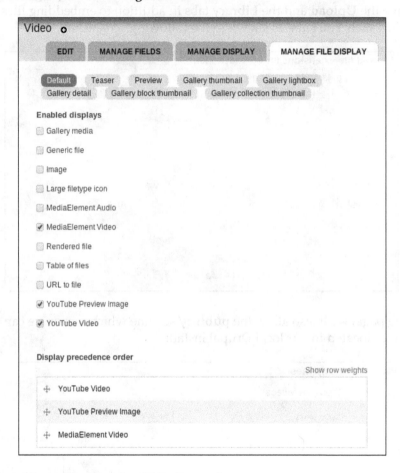

You will notice that once the **MediaElement Video** display has been enabled, it also added **Display settings** for it, much like we had seen with the YouTube Video display settings, where we can decide whether it will feature the controls bar, width and height dimensions, and possibly a download link too as shown in the following screenshot:

When you're satisfied with this configuration click on **Save**. Do the same process for the **Teaser, Preview, Gallery Thumbnail**, and **Gallery Lightbox** tabs too, as this will serve us later. For the **Gallery Thumbnail** display you might want to adjust the width and height settings to match the image style for it too.

All configuration is finished and we're ready to play locally hosted video files. Create a new Vidz content, you'll notice that when selecting media you're now able to upload a new file or choose from existing files in your library, along with the option to still embed videos from YouTube.

Once you have submitted the video, you can see already MediaElement's video player in action when saving the video format fields that we've setup earlier:

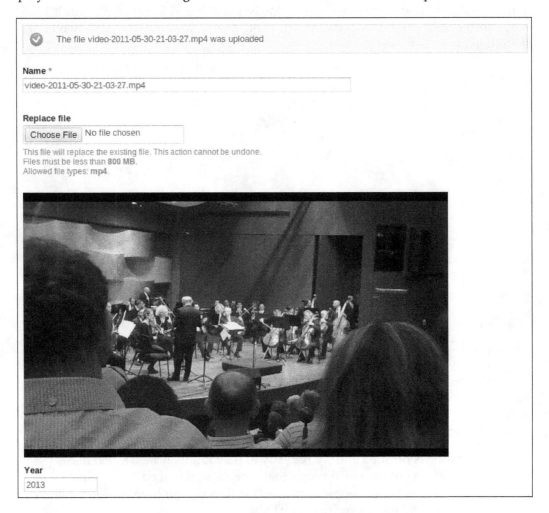

And finally when saving this Vidz entry you will also be able to play the video, whether in full node view or in teaser or preview modes (if you have indeed enabled the video player display format when we've set this up).

Galleries and playlists

Just as we've seen with pictures, we can create collections of videos and put them in a gallery, with slideshow, and so on. Unlike pictures, with videos it comes handy to provide a playlist where users can create their own personal watch list.

We will explore a couple of ways to enhance plain video content by adding galleries and playlists features.

Video galleries

Much like with images and thanks to a seamless integration of the MediaElement module, whether it's third-party hosted videos or locally hosted videos, we can make use of the Media Galleries module to create video galleries too.

First, we need to make sure that the Galleries content type which the Media Galleries module created is able to support video media. While it's possible to create yet another Galleries content type that will be used for video galleries, for simplicity's sake we can go ahead and edit the existing Galleries content type, the configuration remains the same.

Navigate to **Structure** | **Content Types** | **Gallery** | **manage fields** and click on **edit** on the **Gallery Media** field (`admin/structure/types/manage/media-gallery/fields/media_gallery_file`) — this is the actual field that is being used when adding any type of media to a gallery. For the **Enabled browser plugins** we can toggle on all required browsing fields but because we want to be able to both upload files as well as embed files from third parties which is basically toggling on all of the options, it's ok to leave none of them toggled on, as it is by default, which means that all of them will appear. If the **Allowed file extensions for uploaded files** field is missing video formats you'll need to specify them. Make sure **Allowed remote media types** field has the **Video** option toggled on, and **Allowed URI schemes** field allows for both **public://** and **youtube://** URI schemes.

If you hadn't configured the MediaElement Video display format to render in the **MANAGE FILE DISPLAY** page (`/admin/structure/file-types/manage/video/file-display`) as we did earlier when setting up the MediaElement module then consult the *Uploading videos and playing them* section and make sure it's enabled.

Let's begin by creating a new gallery for band videos at **Add Content** | **Gallery** (`/node/add/media-gallery`). Add a **Title** and customize the gallery settings, look and feel to your liking and click on **Save**. Now that the gallery has been created, it's empty so click on **Add media** and try adding both an upload video and later on a YouTube video.

Congratulations! Finally this should look as follows, including a slideshow and lightbox functionality when clicking on each video:

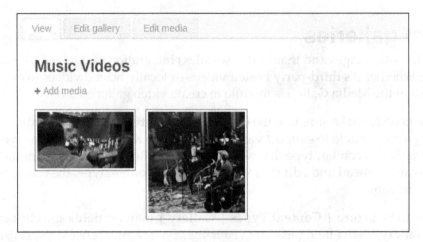

 It doesn't really matter what type of media is involved, pictures, video or audio, you can really blend all of them together in the same gallery.

Video playlists

The MediaElement module doesn't have built-in support for playlists, so we'll be using Drupal's MediaFront module, which is based on the Open Source Media Player library (`http://www.mediafront.org/osmplayer`) and out of the box provides great customizing capabilities, support for playing both video and audio, and fallback for Flash. All of which, makes it a pretty decent selection as our media player.

Installing the MediaFront module

Download the MediaFront's module 7.x-2.x's branch (`http://drupal.org/project/mediafront`), unpack and enable the module as always, via your favorite method of installation. The module ships with some sub modules so make sure you enable all of the following: **MediaFront** and **Open Standards Media Player**, both of which are listed in the **Modules** page (`/admin/modules`).

The player which MediaFront displays for media content can be customized to an overwhelming degree. It allows to create player configurations, called presets, which can be assigned to different content types, their fields, or even display modes. For example, you may want to display a very small player window, without any controls and have a specific look and feel, all of which when you're viewing a teaser's node view. But when viewing a full node's view you'd probably want to see it in a bigger screen size, maybe even play a video file before playing the actual uploaded video (for example, playing a sponsored commercial), and so on.

Configuring the MediaFront module

When the MediaFront module installs, it doesn't create any such preset by default so we'll need to create one before doing anything else. Navigate to **Structure | MediaFront Presets | ADD PRESET** (/admin/structure/mediafront/add) and give the preset a name and click on **Next** as shown in the following screenshot:

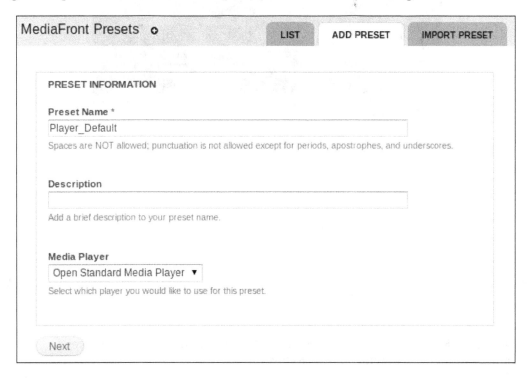

Moving on to the next screen we see the many configuration options that the preset allows to set for this player:

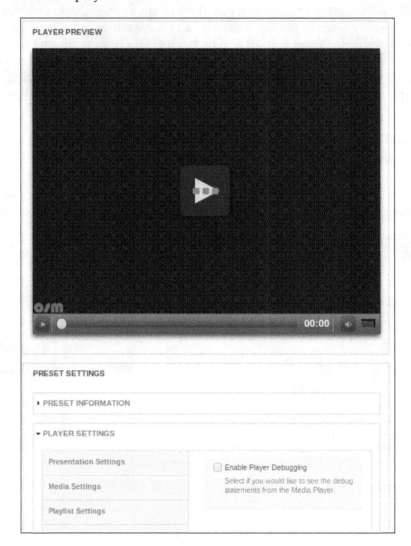

The **PLAYER SETTINGS** field set features the important parts of the player configuration, some of which are as follows :

- **Presentation Settings**: Due to MediaFront's integration with jQuery UI it allows setting the player's theme to match that of jQuery's. It further more allows to create custom templates, as well as other player presentation options.

- **Media Settings**: It define the behavior of the played media, whether to play a specific media file before or after the main media file (that which is contained in the upload field), as well as the default volume and default loading options, for example, **Auto Load** will have the browser request the media file from the server, which may not be the best thing to do in terms of bandwidth consideration if you're going to use this preset for displaying a list of 10 or more items.

- **Playlist Settings**: It enhances the playlists support, look, and feel, and play behavior, such as whether media files should automatically play when a previous file ends, or if the playlist should randomly selects media files to play.

There are more settings which you can easily browse through and customize to your own extent.

We will create two presets which we will make use of later on: one preset will be a large video player view so it's ok to leave the defaults sizes (100 percent width and 450px height) and the second preset will be used as a thumbnail player so that it doesn't take a lot of screen real-estate and we can display a listing of more than just one or two (you can probably name that second preset `player_thumbnail`).

Once you're satisfied with the player settings click on **Save Preset** and we'll get on with our demo.

Creating a content type for the MediaFront videos

To demonstrate the use of the MediaFront's module, we'll create a new content type called Concertz which will list concert music videos. For our video field, we won't use Media module's Multimedia asset field type, but rather the **File** field and set the widget type to **Media file selector** (so we can still make use of the Media's uploading and library browser type interface). The field's configuration should look as shown in the following screenshot:

LABEL	MACHINE NAME	FIELD TYPE	WIDGET	OPERATIONS
Title	title	Node module element		
Body	body	Long text and summary	Text area with a summary	edit delete
Video	field_concert_video	File	Media file selector	edit delete

When you're ready click on **Save** followed by another **Save field settings** for the intermediate field settings page.

Due to the way that the MediaFront module attaches to content type's in the field level, you may notice that we've got some new configuration options now that is, **MEDIAFRONT SETTINGS**. We can choose out of a few of options to let MediaFront figure out what kind of media is this **File** field all about, so for our case we'll set it to **Media**, and make sure the default **Media Content** option is set for the **Media Type** field as shown in the following screenshot:

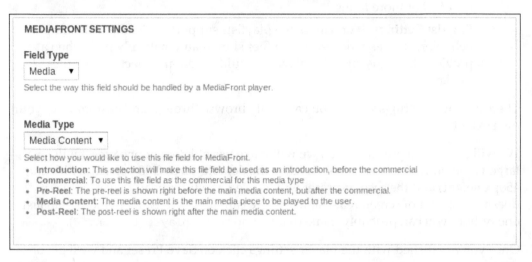

Also, make sure that the **Allowed remote media types** field has the **Video** option set, and **Allowed file extensions for uploaded files** field has some videos formats listed, some options are MP3, MOV, MP4, M4A, M4V, MPEG, AVI, OGG, OGA, and OGV. When you're finished, click on **Save**.

Using the file field we added our Concertz field for us to upload files but we haven't yet told Drupal how to render this field. If you can recall from previous sections, without specific display configuration, an uploaded file will simply show up as a link to download it. So let's fix that – navigate to the **MANAGE DISPLAY** tab of the Concertz content type (/admin/structure/types/manage/concertz/display) and set the **FORMAT** column for the **Video** field to use **MediaFront Player** and then click on the gear icon to configure the settings for format and choose the preset that we created. Finally, the **MANAGE DISPLAY** tab should look as follows:

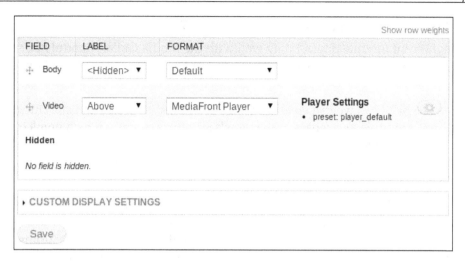

After saving our new Concertz content type let's create a few content items with it which will compile our playlist. A successful configuration will yield the MediaFront's video player rendering when the node is viewed as follows:

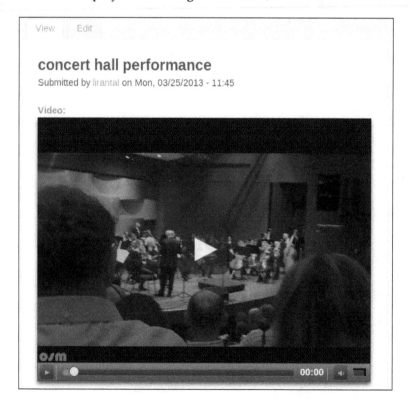

Creating a Views-based playlist

The MediaFront module doesn't play well with the Media Gallery module but that's fine, as at least it plays pretty well with the rest of Drupal's, and specifically with the Views module.

With the use of Views we can create galleries of videos, or even playlists. Due to MediaFront's module awareness of the view's structure, such as which items it is displaying, as well as which fields are being displayed, it enables a very aware integration of filters and other view handlers to be used in a view and much associated with the actual content that's being displayed.

We'll create a view that lists all Concertz content type items in a grid view mode. It will make use of the player_thumbnail preset we created but we'll also add MediaFront's global player handler to play all the videos in the view. By doing that, we actually turn the view listing to be the playlist itself. To begin, we'll navigate to **Structure | Views | Add new view** (/admin/structure/views/add) to add the view and fill-in the basic settings, such as the name of the view, what kind of content type are we listing, and the display format which we set to **Grid** of **fields** instead of the default option. Click on **Continue & edit** to further fine-tune the view's settings as shown in the following screenshot:

By default, the grid display format uses four columns, which is too large for our theme so in the **FORMAT** field set we clicked on **Settings** next to the **Grid** option and modified the **Number of columns** to two instead of four.

You can click on **Save** now and see a preview of how the view will look like in the bottom of the page. At this point it lists just the basic fields of each item, we'll add the Video field there too so that it adds a bit more color to our view listing.

> Instead of having a player render for each content item, you could also create another field for image uploads to Concertz content type to be used as picture covers for the videos, and then list the grid with the picture cover.

In **FIELDS** field set the node's **Title** field is added by default when listing fields, so click on the **add** button to the right and toggle on the **Content: Video** option which appears in **node:concertz** content type. When the new field settings show up toggle off the **Create a label** checkbox and we'll modify the **Formatter** to use **MediaFront Player** and **player_thumbnail** option for the **MediaFront Presets** setting. In the **MEDIAFRONT SETTINGS** field-set, toggle on the **Link to Player** checkbox and set the **Media** option for the **Field Type** setting, as well as the **Media Content** for the **Media Type** setting. After clicking the **Apply** button you can already see the preview updates to list the playable videos.

> If you had wanted to create just a gallery of videos it would have been enough to simply stop here, customize the view if you'd like, even customize the MediaFront preset player too and you've got yourself a videos gallery.

Next thing we'll do is add the MediaFront Player handler to the header part of the view and by doing that we're adding a player which is aware of all listed items and will play them one by one, without requiring user interaction.

In the **HEADER** field set click on the **add** button and choose the first option **Global: MediaFront Player**. In the **MEDIAFRONT SETTINGS** field-set, set the **Media** option for the **Field Type** setting, as well as the **Media Content** for the **Media Type** setting and click on **Apply**.

Save the view, and we're ready to navigate to the new view by browsing to
/music-videos, which is the path that was set for us automatically by the view,
based on the title we choose for it. It should look as follows, and you'll notice that
the bigger player, moves to the next item in the view when the current one ends.

Summary

In this chapter we've explored the myriad of options to add videos media to our
website. We have learned about integrating with third-party video-hosting websites
like YouTube, as well as creating our very own YouTube-like video sharing platform
by enabling users to upload videos to our Drupal hosted website. We have further
explored options to customize video uploads with new fields, using media player
libraries, and creating play lists and galleries.

In the next chapter we will proceed to another type of media resource on the
Internet, audio content, and find out how to integrate it with Drupal websites.

6
Audio Capabilities

While the web has been growing in regards to the amount of visual content, in the form of pictures and movies of all sorts, audio content is under-estimated.

Music streaming has been quietly preserving it's spot on the web, such as Internet radio stations or social networks such as SoundCloud, which enable users to share their own music and collaborate with one another.

In this chapter we will cover:

- Adding playable audio fields
- Using media libraries such as MediaElement to play audio
- Understanding HTML5 Audio element and making use of the audio JavaScript API
- Learning about the ID3 standard for audio files metadata and how to make use of this to enrich information on MP3 audio file uploads
- Leveraging ID3 metadata to persist MP3 audio file in Drupal fields storage by creating your own custom module

We have previously known music around the Internet with the long-living MP3 format, which is used for distributing audio content among peers. It has evolved due to the need to share, which was quite impossible with the raw WAV format and most default file extensions among many operating systems. Back then, bandwidth wasn't as generous as today, with a ratio of about 10 megabytes for 1 minute for CD quality sound that took its toll on Internet speeds. This problem gave rise to some compression formats, yet the popular MP3 prevailed and became an un-official standard among users. Its one thing to share audio files, but bringing audio content as a streaming media to the web is quite another. As with most things pre-HTML5, it required browser plugins and as we've seen already with HTML5, we can make use of the spec's `<audio>` tag to play some formats which are being advised as standard audio codecs and formats. That, coupled with leveraging a JavaScript API which browsers expose to interact with the media in play, provide a richer and more streamlined experience for both developers as well as end-users.

Supported audio formats

The HTML5 spec is a bit vague on proposing recommended audio formats (remember that it's still a draft). While at some point, **Vorbis** format was supposed to be a sought after standard due to it being free of patents and such, the popularity of formats such as MP3 might actually make them the official standard. For the time being, while Chrome is now leading the browser charts and it supports a wide variety of formats (Ogg Vorbis, WAVs, MP3, AAC, WebM, and others), it is probably best to provide audio files in both Vorbis as well as MP3 or AAC to make sure all browsers support playing the audio content.

Browsers support matrix for the `<audio>` field formats provided by Wikipedia (`http://en.wikipedia.org/wiki/HTML5_Audio`), as shown in the following screenshot:

Browser	Operating system	Formats supported by different web browsers					
		Ogg Vorbis	WAV PCM	MP3	AAC	WebM Vorbis	Ogg Opus
Google Chrome	All supported	9	Yes	Yes	Yes	Yes	25
Internet Explorer	Windows	No	No	9.0	9.0	No	No
Mozilla Firefox (Gecko)	All supported	3.5 (1.9.1)	3.5 (1.9.1)	21.0 (21.0), Windows only	21.0 (21.0), Windows only	4.0 (2.0)	15.0 (15.0)
Opera	All supported	10.50	11.00	No	No	10.60	No
Safari	OS X	No	3.1	3.1	3.1	No	No

Enabling audio play

Our first task will be to enable audio uploads with audio play capabilities. Formerly, this was accomplished using a dedicated audio field type which third-party modules provided to extend content types using the **Content Construction Kit (CCK)** framework.

We've already been using the Media module for pictures and videos and we can make use of it to provide our audio content as well. Doing so will allow us to manage all of our media resources in the same place, using the media browser. Keeping in mind that the Media module is only about setting the grounds for managing media resources, we will need enable a media player that will be able to stream those audio formats. Luckily, both MediaElement and MediaFront provide this support using HTML5's `<audio>` tag.

Adding a new content type

Tracks will be the name of our new content type, for users to be able to upload their songs, vocals, instrumental music tracks, or audio content in general. Once uploaded, they will be able to play it just as if it were a video.

 Note that you may need to adjust your PHP settings `upload_max_filesize` and `post_max_size` to allow large file uploads. These settings are usually placed in the site-wide `php.ini` file (you can find out where it is located on your filesystem by running the command `php --ini`).

To create our Tracks content type, we'll navigate to **Structure | Content types | + Add content type** (`/admin/structure/types/add`) and name it **Tracks**, then click on **Save**, and add fields. We'll name our new audio field simply `Track`, choose the **Multimedia asset** as FIELD TYPE and **Media file selector** as WIDGET and click on **Save**. Our content type should be structured as follows:

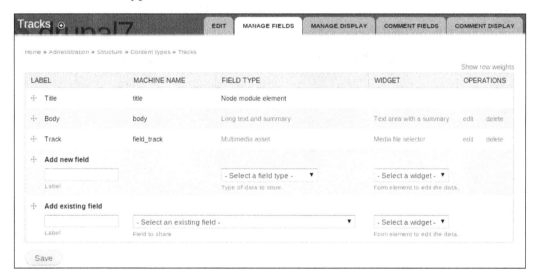

We can continue to edit our new field settings (`/admin/structure/types/manage/tracks/fields/field_track`), where we'll need to make sure that the **Allowed file extensions for uploaded files** field lists the audio extensions we want to support. Probably, most common of which are MP3, WAV, and OGA (the OGA extension is basically an OGG container for the Vorbis format with an audio stream only).

Allowed file extensions for uploaded files *
mp3, wav, mov, mp4, m4a, oga, ogg
Separate extensions with a space or comma and do not include the leading dot.

And also make sure the **Allowed remote media types** field has the **Audio** option set.

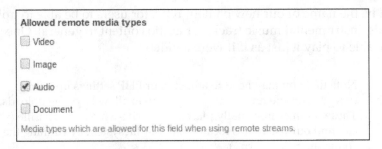

That's basically it, click on **Save** and we're done with setting up the field settings, but we still need to make sure that along with the audio media field it will bind to a media player that will render the file into a player widget.

Navigate to **Structure | File types | Audio | manage file display** (`/admin/structure/file-types/manage/audio/file-display`) and we'll need to choose the display formatters for an audio media field type. Go ahead and toggle on the **MediaElement Audio** option.

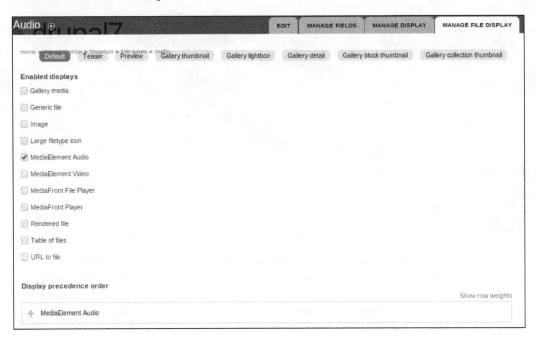

It will be added as the only enabled display, if this is a fresh new configuration, and populate the settings with defaults such as 300 by 30 pixels player widget with audio controls and no download link for the actual audio file.

The end result should look as follows with the MediaElement's audio widget player rendering the file as an actual player.

Customizing audio nodes

Let's break-out from the common module usage of audio player widgets and their configurations and customize the node view for a couple of use cases which can definitely evolve to complete web and mobile apps, if you really put your mind to it.

We will leverage HTML5 Audio field, along with some JavaScript code to manipulate the audio playback, and tie this into the node view rendering within Drupal.

Aiming for multi-channel playback

When music is recorded, each instrument is placed in it's own channel, forming a layered and isolated instance for each one. This can then be used for easily adding or deleting instruments later on when processing the song, or possibly modifying a single channel's sound during the song, without affecting everything else. This is very similar to how drawings are often sketched in layers.

Imagine if we could create a sort of multi-channel player web application where musicians could upload their tracks, each channel of recording in it's own file, and users can then play the track channel by channel, possibly muting the vocals and singing along the played audio track, just like a karaoke machine.

To first go about doing that we'll need to enable our Tracks content type to allow more than one media resource upload widgets. Navigate to **Structure | Content types | Tracks | manage fields** and click on **edit** on the **Track** field (`/admin/structure/types/manage/tracks/fields/field_track`). Scroll down to **TRACK FIELD SETTINGS** and make sure the **Number of values** setting is set to **Unlimited** (or the amount of channels you wish to allow, for the sake of the example an unlimited value is okay) and click on **Save settings**.

Once that's done, we can edit or add a new Tracks content item and see that it's allowing multiple (actually, unlimited) audio tracks to be submitted and then displayed and played in the node view:

Viewing the node we created with multiple audio tracks, we can see that it displays the audio player for each of them, but if you try to play all of them together you will notice that this is not working. When one player starts, it stops the rest of the widget players (technically, it pauses them) and it's not really aligned with our use case of being able to play multiple audio tracks simultaneously and allowing users to pause or change volume levels to a single track when other tracks are being played.

To this end, we'll avoid using the MediaElement library and leverage the HTML5 Audio standard to simply allow the browser to render its own player according to the specs. For this purpose, and to serve yet another use case to come along, we will customize the Tracks node content type theme with our own version.

To override the node's theme with our own code, we will create the following file in our theme's directory `sites/all/themes/corolla/node--tracks.tpl.php`. If you have decided to work with another theme (the default theme name is Bartik), you will need to create the same file in that theme directory and add the following code to the file:

```
<article id="node-<?php print $node->nid; ?>" class="<?php print
$classes; ?> clearfix"<?php print $attributes; ?>>
  <div class="node-inner">

    <?php print $unpublished; ?>

    <?php print render($title_prefix); ?>
    <?php if ($title || $display_submitted): ?>
      <header<?php print $header_attributes; ?>>

        <?php if ($title): ?>
          <h1<?php print $title_attributes; ?>>
            <?php if (!$page): ?>
              <a href="<?php print $node_url; ?>" rel="bookmark"><?php
                print $title; ?></a>
            <?php elseif ($page): ?>
              <?php print $title; ?>
            <?php endif; ?>
          </h1>
        <?php endif; ?>

        <?php if ($display_submitted): ?>
          <p class="submitted"><?php print $submitted; ?></p>
        <?php endif; ?>

      </header>
    <?php endif; ?>
    <?php print render($title_suffix); ?>
```

Until this point, the preceding code snippet is taken from the stock `node.tpl.php` file and is basically responsible for the generic parts of header, submission date, and node title.

Next, we will introduce our own code. It begins by inspecting the $content variable for a field called field_track, which is the internal name our Tracks field was created under, and counts the number of items in its #items array. Using this, we can print the number of audio content that were uploaded. We then continue to loop through the array of items and using information that is stored there, we create an <audio> HTML5 element, specifying the source of the file on our server, as well as providing a download link for users to simply right-click on and save the audio file if they wish to.

```php
<?php
  // Grab all of the uploaded audio files. Using this
  // information, we later on print the amount of audio channels
  // for this Tracks content item.
  $items_count = 0;
  if (isset($content['field_track']['#items']))
    $items_count = count($content['field_track']['#items']);
?>
<h4>
<?php echo $items_count?> audio channels in this track compilation:
</h4>

<?php
  $count = 0;

  // Loop through the Tracks' field items array to grab the
  // information stored for each item.
  if (isset($content['field_track']['#items'])):
    foreach ($content['field_track']['#items'] as $item):
      // While the $item['file']->uri holds Drupal's generic file
      // uri for this file (such as public://some_file_name.mp3)
      // we need to convert this to an actual valid URI and
      // scheme to apply as the file source for the audio
      // elements

      $filename = file_create_url($item['file']->uri);
      $fid = 'fid'.$item['file']->fid;

      // Increment generic audio channel count
      $count++;
?>

<!--
Using the populated $filename and $fid variables we can set an HTML5
audio element, along with the thematic break <hr> tag to separate the
audio fields to give it a channel look
-->
```

```
<hr>
Channel <?php echo $count; ?>:
<audio src="<?php echo $filename?>" controls id="<?php echo $fid?>">
</audio> <a href="<?php echo $filename?>"> Download audio channel </a>

<?php
  endforeach;
  endif;
?>
<hr>
```

And finally, we will alter the footer part of the stock `node.tpl.php` file to comment
the rendering of content (as you can see in the highlightedd part of the following
code), and leave the footer part as it is, for information such as comments or any
node links that modules extend.

We comment this highlighted part of the code because the `$content` variable holds a
lot of information regarding the content that is being displayed for rendering and we
are not interested in presenting it to the user.

```
<div<?php print $content_attributes; ?>>
<?php print $user_picture; ?>
<?php

  hide($content['comments']);
  hide($content['links']);
  /**
  * Commenting the $content variable so that modules that plug
  into the node fields do not render (such as the MediaElement)
  and we basically remove any information Drupal has to print for
  this node.
  print render($content);
  */


?>
</div>

<?php if ($links = render($content['links'])): ?>
  <nav<?php print $links_attributes; ?>><?php print $links;
    ?></nav>
<?php endif; ?>

<?php print render($content['comments']); ?>

</div>
</article>
```

As with most things in Drupal, it's possible to accomplish a task in more than one way. One way to override node templates is to make use of the templating system which seeks out the template file to use for displaying a node by going through the most specific occurrence to the most generic. For example, to display the Tracks content type node view, which is saved as the `tracks` machine-readable name within Drupal, it will seek out a file named `node--<NODE_ID>.tpl.php`, then `node--tracks.tpl.php`, and finally, `node.tpl.php` as the most generic node view. It searches for these files in the currently used theme's directory, which in our case happens to be the Corolla theme that we installed earlier in the book. There are other ways to theme a node, such as implementing one of the theme_preprocess functions and others.

After saving the new node template file with its code content, make sure to clear your Drupal's cache so that the theming system gets rebuilt and is aware of the new template. Navigate to **Configuration | Development | Performance** and click on **Clear all caches** (`/admin/config/development/performance`) which does the job. Then visiting that multiple audio content items node that we created earlier, it should look as follows:

Our customized node template now shows the built-in web browser player widget (the look-and-feel may differ from browser to browser), that allows us to play each audio file that was uploaded. Moreover, it's possible to play the audio tracks all together without one of them stopping the other one from play.

Because we have already got a JavaScript media library installed and ready to use, we can make use of it very simply by altering the node template and applying the correct JavaScript to instantiate the MediaElement Audio player for each of the <audio> elements we have. Before adjusting the code, we will make sure that the MediaElement library is being loaded site-wide, which means that its JavaScript classes will be available for us. Navigate to **Configuration** | **Media** | **MediaElement. js** (/admin/config/media/mediaelement) and toggle on **Enable MediaElement.js site wide** and click on **Save configuration**.

Next, append the following code before or after our modified highlighted code in the node--tracks.tpl.php file:

```
<script>
jQuery(document).ready(function($) {
<?php
  foreach ($content['field_track']['#items'] as $item):
    $fid = 'fid'.$item['file']->fid;
?>
 $('#<?php echo $fid ?>').mediaelementplayer({features: ['playpause',
'loop', 'current', 'progress', 'duration', 'volume']});
<?php
  endforeach;
?>
});
</script>
```

The code snippet is made up of both PHP and JavaScript. The PHP part is being used to loop through the audio content items, exactly as we did before, to get the file IDs for each audio element (that is also why we've made use of the ID attribute earlier for the audio elements). Inside that loop, we instantiate the MediaElementPlayer object which turns each of the <audio> elements into a themed and controlled widget using that JavaScript library.

The result should look as follows with the MediaElement Audio player widget being rendered, instead of the browser's own widget:

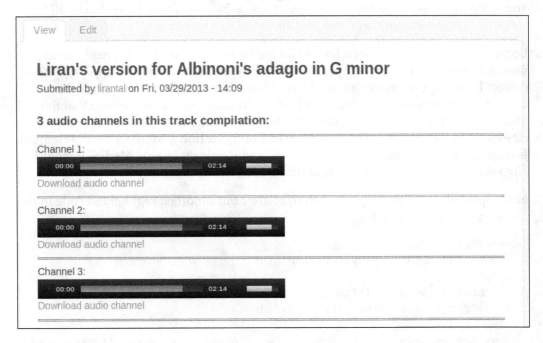

Knowing how to do this, you can make use of any other JavaScript media library and render your audio nodes with custom players.

Some suggestions to build on this idea:

- With the use of external JavaScript audio libraries, you can add more sound effects such as fade in and fade out, sound altering effects, and so on. This further enriches the experience of user's in-browser remixing of audio.

- Add social features such as allowing several users to collaborate on a single track, each contributing his or her own audio channels. For example, to create the virtual band web applications, one user can provide the drums background music, while another guitar player user can then build some rhythm channel to add to that and so on.

Creating a drum machine

Building further on HTML5's audio element, we can make use of the JavaScript API to manipulate the played media. Our next use case will be to create a drum machine web application, where users can upload their own drum-kit audio samples to compose their own drum machine, and then be able to click-away their drum beats.

Because we're using HTML5, the drum machine template will be rendering on mobile devices too and enabling us to grow our audience reach.

It's possible to create yet another node content type, much like the Tracks content type that we created, but since we have it already and even provided custom node template for displaying it, we will make use of this asset again for the drum machine use case.

To begin, we need some sound samples to work with. While it's possible to just put any song you might have already existing use on your computer, your experience will be much more real for this use case if you actually use drum sound samples. They are easily found on the web just by Googling the phrase `free drum machine samples` or alike which will yield at least one website where you can freely download a few WAVs. One such site is `http://www.freedrumkits.net`. After gaining a few drum WAVs, create a new Tracks content item and upload some of them.

While we can use the same in-browser widget player or even a JavaScript media library, there are a few inherent limitations with that which don't suit us:

- An audio player widget doesn't make a good user experience for users as we don't really care that much about the progress bar, the time measures or even that much about the volume. If we consider our mobile users too then operating an audio player widget for drums becomes a terrible task in terms of user interface.

- The play or pause button has no justification because we never really need to pause the drum sound. Moreover, we need an interface that allows the user to click on it several times, where upon each click it will rewind the sound sample and play it again. This way the user can "hit" a drum multiple times.

Due to the previous points, it seems that we need to change the in-browser widget with something else as well as add some JavaScript code to respond to drum hits.

Design-wise it would have probably been better to make use of actual drum element pictures (such as a snare, a hi-hat, and so on) in collaboration with proper JavaScript and CSS code to really style it, but we can get right to business with using an HTML's button element and a bit of inline CSS to create our drums' "hit" interface.

Once again, we will customize the `sites/all/themes/corolla/node--tracks. tpl.php` file with our own code that will draw clickable HTML buttons, which makes use of JavaScript code to rewind the sound loop and play it:

We begin by copying over the header part of the code from the stock `node.tpl.php` file:

```
<article id="node-<?php print $node->nid; ?>" class="<?php print
$classes; ?> clearfix"<?php print $attributes; ?>>
  <div class="node-inner">

    <?php print $unpublished; ?>

    <?php print render($title_prefix); ?>
    <?php if ($title || $display_submitted): ?>
      <header<?php print $header_attributes; ?>>

        <?php if ($title): ?>
          <h1<?php print $title_attributes; ?>>
            <?php if (!$page): ?>
              <a href="<?php print $node_url; ?>" rel="bookmark"><?php
                print $title; ?></a>
            <?php elseif ($page): ?>
              <?php print $title; ?>
            <?php endif; ?>
          </h1>
        <?php endif; ?>

        <?php if ($display_submitted): ?>
          <p class="submitted"><?php print $submitted; ?></p>
        <?php endif; ?>

      </header>
    <?php endif; ?>
    <?php print render($title_suffix); ?>
```

Then, the following JavaScript code snippet receives the ID attribute's value of an `<audio>` element as an HTML object to work with and if successful, it rewinds it back to the beginning of the audio sound and plays it.

```
<script>
/**
 * JavaScript function to rewind and play an audio element
 * @param string the HTML element's id attribute value
 * @return bool FALSE on errors
 */
function play_audio_sound(element_id) {
  if (!element_id) {
```

```
      return FALSE;
    }

    // Check if the browser supports HTML5's audio element
    try {

      // Create an audio object variable from the element's id
      var audio_object = document.getElementById(element_id);

      // Rewind the audio sound to the start and play the audio
      audio_object.currentTime = 0;
      audio_object.play();
    }
    catch (exception) {
      alert('there was an error playing the audio: '
        + exception.message);
      return FALSE;
    }
  }
}
</script>
```

Our next PHP code, which is similar to the multi-channel use case, loops through the audio upload items and extracts the filename and file ID as well as the file's name that the user provided, when uploading the file. It creates both an <audio> element as well as a <button> element that calls our JavaScript function to play the audio.

```php
<?php
  foreach ($content['field_track']['#items'] as $item):
    $filename = file_create_url($item['file']->uri);
    $fid = 'fid'.$item['file']->fid;
    $file_name = $item['file']->filename;
?>

<audio src="<?php echo $filename?>" id="<?php echo $fid?>"> </audio>

<button onClick="javascript:play_audio_sound('<?php echo $fid ?>');"
  style="height:80px; width:120px;"><?php echo $file_name ?></button>

<?php
  endforeach;
?>
```

Notice how we stripped the controls attribute from the <audio> element this time, as we don't want the browser to render the audio player widget for each item. Moreover, while the onClick JavaScript function handler is being used here, we recognize that this may not be modern JavaScript example, especially with the use of jQuery and Drupal behavior pattern but it's being used for the sake of simplicity. The source code available for this book offers better JavaScript implementations.

And finally, the part left in this template file is related to the footer. We modify it slightly by commenting out the $content variable printing as we're not interested in this:

```
<div<?php print $content_attributes; ?>>
<?php print $user_picture; ?>
<?php

  hide($content['comments']);
  hide($content['links']);
  // print render($content);
?>
</div>

<?php if ($links = render($content['links'])): ?>
  <nav<?php print $links_attributes; ?>><?php print $links;
    ?></nav>
<?php endif; ?>

<?php print render($content['comments']); ?>

    </div>
  </article>
```

There is no need to clear the cache for the template to pick up this file if you've done this already in the previous chapter, otherwise please do so at /admin/config/development/performance and navigate back to view the node in its new theme, it should look as follows:

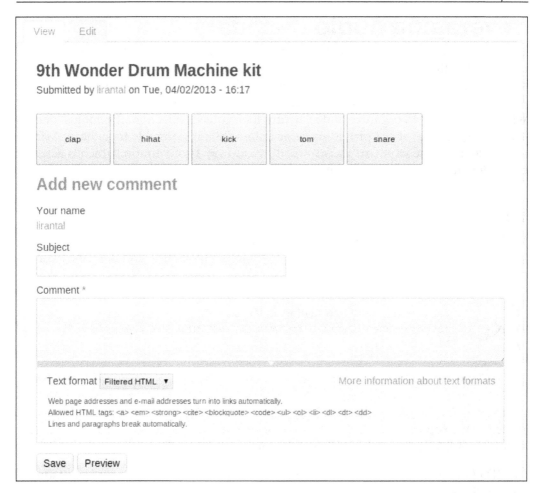

Some ideas to further build on this:

- Style the user interface to provide a much more slick and intuitive experience. For example, you can randomly color the buttons or better yet replace them with a picture of a drum instrument.

- Allow users to collaborate and create their own drum kits and contribute to one another.

- When using JavaScript to call the play function, it's then possible to record these events and in turn record a history of all clicked events, which really means to record the drum sounds that were played and re-use it as a beat-machine or re-play a recorded rhythm over and over in a loop.

Leveraging audio metadata

With regards to audio, metadata has long been a useful addition which was directly associated with MP3 audio files. Back then, the MP3 format was heavily used to store audio files but it lacked a way to describe the file's content. Information such as artist name, track title, album name, year of release, and genre, are powerful assets which allow users to organize and structure their music collection. It's not just about organizing but also about providing basic data. While it's possible to name an MP3 audio file using the `<artist name>-<song name>.mp3` convention, which is actually the widely used format, it's not really efficient.

ID3

With this problem among the community, came rise of the ID3 standard as a way to attach metadata to MP3 files, enabling users to tag their files, and describe their audio tracks using dedicated fields.

> You can find more information on ID3 tags at `http://id3.org`, `http://getid3.sourceforge.net`, and `http://en.wikipedia.org/wiki/ID3`.

The ID3 standard had re-invented itself numerous times to accommodate demand for better metadata support. One example for this is where ID3v2 was created to enable variable-length fields, as well as support for Unicode characters, all of which placed in the beginning of the file to allow for streaming media services to make use of this metadata without having to seek through the entire file.

The ID3 PHP library, we will work with, is able to do more than just basic metadata fields but also supports the following:

- Reading and writing to other formats than just MP3 such as Ogg Vorbis.
- Reading metadata from video formats such as MKV, AVI, MPEG1, MPEG2, and others, as well as reading from image formats such as JPEGs, PNGs, BMPs, and others.

Installing the ID3 module and library

We will be using a Drupal module called **getID3** as well as a PHP library called getID3, which will aid us in extracting metadata from multimedia files.

We will begin by downloading the ID3 PHP library which is located at `http://www.getid3.org`, simply browse there and make sure you download the latest 1.x stable version (at the time of writing this book it was 1.9.5). Once you've got it, create the directory `sites/all/libraries/getid3` and extract the contents of the getID3 library archive that you downloaded to that directory and extract it there, which should result in the following file being accessible: `sites/all/libraries/getid3/getid3/write.php`.

The getID3 library comes with some working-code demos, documentation, and other resources. To avoid any security issues, you should proceed with deleting the `demos` directory at `sites/all/libraries/getid3/getid3/demos`. To make sure it is definitely not accessible and you removed it correctly, try accessing the URL `/sites/all/libraries/getid3/getid3/demos/demo.browse.php` and make sure it fails to load and render that file.

Download the getID3 Drupal module (`http://drupal.org/project/getid3`) and use the 7.x branch (at the time of writing this book we made use of the 7.x-1.0 version). Once downloaded, enable the module (at `/admin/modules`) and navigate to **Configuration | Media | getID3()** which hosts a very minimal configuration page (`/admin/config/media/getid3`) for the getID3 Drupal module:

---

getID3() ⚙

To use this module you'll need to download the library from the getID3 website and extract the contents into the module's getid3 directory. Currently, the recommended version of the getID3 library is 1.8.2.

Path

    sites/all/libraries/getid3/getid3

The location where getID3() is installed. Relative paths are from the Drupal root directory.

Version

1.9.5-20130220

If you're seeing this it indicates that the getID3 library was found.

☐ Display Warnings

Check this to display the warning messages from the getID3 library when reading and writing ID3 tags. Generally it's a good idea to leave this unchecked, getID3 reports warnings for several trivial problems and the warnings can be confusing to users. This setting can be useful when debugging problems with the ID3 tags.

Save configuration

While it's possible to configure a different path for the getID3 library, in practice this configuration page will actually help you figure out if the library was installed correctly or not using the **Version** field which shows the version it detected.

 We're making use of the getID3 module for Drupal but it's really just a wrapper for instantiating the getID3 library among some other insignificant functionality. If you plan to use the getID3 library in large Drupal-based projects then you're probably better off with only installing the library, in hope of minimizing the amount of Drupal modules the website uses (due to performance reasons).

Preparing custom node template

To build on our Tracks content type using the custom node template we created (sites/all/themes/corolla/templates/node--tracks.tpl.php), we should be able to introduce more information on each file that we list for audio playback, more specifically, this will be metadata information that we pull off from each file using the getID3 library.

To continue from where we left off, we need to adjust back the code for the custom Tracks content type node template to list each audio file along with its player widget (either the built-in browser or the JavaScript library). For that, simply adjust the custom part of the code as follows:

```php
<?php
  $items_count = 0;
  if (isset($content['field_track']['#items']))
    $items_count = count($content['field_track']['#items']);
?>

<h4>
<?php echo $items_count?> audio channels in this track compilation:
</h4>

<?php
  $count = 0;
  if (isset($content['field_track']['#items'])):
    foreach ($content['field_track']['#items'] as $item):
      $filename = file_create_url($item['file']->uri);
      $fid = 'fid'.$item['file']->fid;
      $count++;
?>
```

```
<hr>
Channel <?php echo $count; ?>:
<audio src="<?php echo $filename?>" controls id="<?php echo $fid?>">
</audio> <a href="<?php echo $filename?>"> Download audio channel </a>
<?php
  endforeach;
  endif;
?>
<hr>
```

And also make sure that the `$content` variable is commented so it doesn't get rendered:

```
//      print render($content);
```

If you haven't been using this custom node type template file up to now then after creating and updating it you will need to clear cache to make sure the theming system registers new hooks and accounts for new template files. To do that, navigate to **Configuration | Development | Performance** (`/admin/config/development/performance`) and click on **Clear all caches**.

To confirm we have a working custom template to work with, either navigate back to one of the Tracks content items that we created or create a new one, with a bunch of MP3 audio files (those with ID3 tags preferably) and make sure it displays a player widget and allows you to actually play the files.

Extracting metadata

The getID3 module we installed will allow us to extract metadata from files, based on their path. The actual code that does it is pretty simple:

```
/* getid3_analyze will instantiate a getid3 object and provide the
constructor with a path for the file, existing and accessible on the
file system.

$file is assumed to be a Drupal's $file object which contains the uri
information that drupal_realpath() makes use of to resolve to real
file system path for that file.
*/
$file_metadata = getid3_analyze(drupal_realpath($file->uri));
```

That single line of code will extract metadata, given a `$file` Drupal object. One place to make use of it is inside our `foreach()` loop where we go through all the uploaded audio files and extract their information. Such as:

```php
<?php
  foreach ($content['field_track']['#items'] as $item):
    $filename = file_create_url($item['file']->uri);
    $fid = 'fid'.$item['file']->fid;
    $count++;

    // Extrat file metadata
    $file_metadata  = getid3_analyze(drupal_realpath($item['file']-
>uri));
  ?>
```

In this loop, we have the `$item` array which populates each of the `$file` object through the `file` array key.

We're now ready to extract metadata from the audio files we uploaded and we can assume that there are some metadata fields, but how do we know which fields we are able to extract and which fields are we interested in?

While you can go through the documentation or test the ID3 library on audio files outside of the Drupal, I would like to introduce a simple way to debug data to the page output, strictly to provide context as to how we learned about the metadata fields, it is in no way a method for debugging your code.

Drupal 7 introduced a convenient way of debugging data using the `debug()` function, where modules can hook into and do things such as pipe the output to a log file, send it over the network to a log server, and so on. By default, it makes use of the status message systems and anything you debug will be printed out to the screen in the form of a status message. Due to the use of the status message systems, any output from that function will only be presented in the next page refresh (this is related to session messages, but we won't go into that now).

To print out the metadata, we will simply make use of the `debug()` function:

```php
<?php
  foreach ($content['field_track']['#items'] as $item):
    $filename = file_create_url($item['file']->uri);
    $fid = 'fid'.$item['file']->fid;
    $count++;

    // Extract file metadata
    $file_metadata  = getid3_analyze(drupal_realpath($item['file']-
      >uri));
    // Print $file_metadata array to the screen
    debug($file_metadata);
  ?>
```

After saving the file, you will need to refresh the Tracks content item you chose to view, twice probably, for the debug output to kick in. Once you do so, you should see a lot of debugging information printed to the page:

```
drupal7

⊘   • Debug: id3 information:
      array (
        'GETID3_VERSION' => '1.9.5-20130220',
        'filesize' => 13416639,
        'filename' => '01. Cold Day In Hell_0.mp3',
        'filepath' => '/www/sites/drupal7/sites/default/files',
        'filenamepath' => '/www/sites/drupal7/sites/default/files
      /01. Cold Day In Hell_0.mp3',
        'avdataoffset' => 2112,
        'avdataend' => 13416511,
        'fileformat' => 'mp3',
        'audio' =>
        array (
          'dataformat' => 'mp3',
          'channels' => 2,
          'sample_rate' => 44100,
          'bitrate' => 320000,
          'channelmode' => 'joint stereo',
          'bitrate_mode' => 'cbr',
          'codec' => 'LAME',
          'encoder' => 'LAME3.98r',
          'lossless' => false,
          'encoder_options' => '--preset insane',
          'compression_ratio' => 0.22675736961451,
```

This part can be deleted. Do we really need to mention the entire thing?

As you can see in your debug output, that's quite a long list of fields and their values, adding up to a bloat of information about each audio file.

You can pick and choose any of them to display, for this example, I've gone ahead with the following: artist, title, album, year, and song track time length. Lets update our code to accommodate for the change of getting this metadata:

```php
<?php
$count = 0;
foreach ($content['field_track']['#items'] as $item):
  $filename = file_create_url($item['file']->uri);
  $fid = 'fid'.$item['file']->fid;
  $count++;

  // Extract file metadata
```

```php
    $file_metadata  = getid3_analyze(drupal_realpath($item['file']-
    >uri));

    // Assign specific metadata fields to array
    $metadata['artist'] = $file_metadata['id3v1']['artist'];
    $metadata['title'] = $file_metadata['id3v1']['title'];
    $metadata['album'] = $file_metadata['id3v1']['album'];
    $metadata['year'] = $file_metadata['id3v1']['year'];
    $metadata['time'] = $file_metadata['playtime_string'];

?>


<hr>
Channel <?php echo $count; ?>:
<audio src="<?php echo $filename?>" controls id="<?php echo $fid?>">
</audio> <a href="<?php echo $filename?>"> Download audio channel </a>
<div>
  <div>
    <label style="display: inline;"> Artist: </label> <?php echo
      $metadata['artist']; ?>
  </div>
  <div>
    <label style="display: inline;"> Title: </label> <?php echo
      $metadata['title']; ?>
  </div>
  <div>
    <label style="display: inline;"> Album: </label> <?php echo
      $metadata['album']; ?> (<?php echo $metadata['year'];?>)
  </div>
  <div>
  <label style="display: inline;"> Time: </label> <?php echo
    $metadata['time']; ?>
  </div>
</div>
<?php
  endforeach;
?>
```

As you can see, we are making use of the array of metadata fields, $metadata, that we extracted in the HTML foreach() loop part, to print this information to the screen.

When working with the 1.x version of the ID3 library, if there was an error in analyzing the provided data, expect to find this information in the returned array's `error` key. Similarly, less critical errors will be returned in the array's `warning` key.

Printing it to the screen will look as follows:

Of course, there is much work to be done in the area of proper HTML5, CSS, and JavaScript, to style this view better, but this paves the way to providing so much more information on media resources that users share, whether they are images, videos, or audio files.

Storing metadata in fields

Extracting metadata on-the-fly, as we did previously with our own custom node template, might be suitable for some situations but it might prove more efficient to create dedicated fields for each metadata item that we're interested in extracting. This, among other advantages, would be better for the following reasons:

- We would not need to analyze files for their metadata information each time they are viewed

- We can make use of these fields later by displaying them in **Views** and filtering based on these items

Our plan to store the metadata fields is to first create the additional fields for the audio file type fields, then to create our own basic module which will populate the fields in the media forms when adding new audio files.

We have seen by now how each media resource such as images, videos, and audio have additional fields defined for them. These fields can be viewed at **Structure | File types** (/admin/structure/file-types) for each file type. For the audio file type, click on **manage fields** on the Audio row (/admin/structure/file-types/ manage/audio/fields). You probably already recognize some fields there, such as the **License settings for this audio** field which showed up when we created or updated our media assets earlier. It is even quite possible that there are some duplicate fields there. Feel free to organize these fields, add others or remove existing, as you see fit. For our use case I have created the required fields for the metadata that we extracted earlier, ending up with the following result:

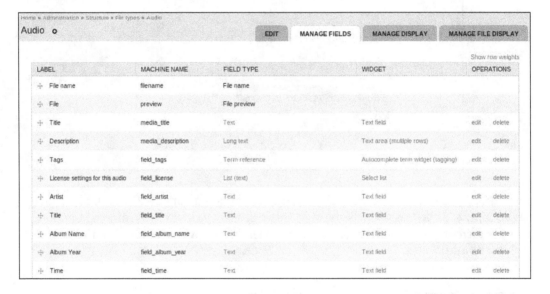

Next up, we'll need to prepare our own very basic module that will extract metadata from the uploaded file and populate the fields we created to store them in. As this is not a Drupal module development book, we will create a very simple and basic module that gets the job done and briefly explains through the code.

A very basic module can be composed of two files only, a `.info` file which provides some generic information (often referred to as metadata too) about the module, and a `.module` file which actually contains the code. Both of these files reside in the module's directory which can be of any name, and their filename prefix is the same. Therefore, let's call our module `store_id3` and proceed to create the module's directory at `sites/all/modules/store_id3`. Starting with our module description metadata, we will create the file `sites/all/modules/store_id3/store_id3.info` and add the following code to it:

```
name = "Store id3"
description = "store_id3 extracts metadata information from media
resources and stores them into Drupal fields"
core = 7.x
files[] = store_id3.module
```

As you can see, the metadata in the form of a `key=value` structure, which provides some information that describes this module. The underlying Drupal system makes use of this information which is used to display the module in the modules administration page.

The second file we need is the actual Drupal code, which we will put in the file `sites/all/modules/store_id3/store_id3.module`:

```php
<?php

/**
 * Implements hook_form_alter().
 */
function store_id3_form_alter(&$form, &$form_state, $form_id) {


  /* Only "jump in" if this is the actual form that we're looking to
     hook into */
  if ($form_id === 'file_entity_edit') {

    /* Get the file id from the $form array and load it into a $file
       object */
    $fid = $form['fid']['#value'];
    $file = file_load($fid);

    if ($file->type === 'audio') {

      // Retrieve file metadata
      $file_metadata = getid3_analyze(drupal_realpath($file->uri));
```

```
        /* Assign the metadata information that we're interested in to
           the $form array */
        $form['field_artist'][LANGUAGE_NONE][0]['value']['#default_
           value'] = $file_metadata['id3v1']['artist'];
        $form['field_title'][LANGUAGE_NONE][0]['value']['#default_
           value'] = $file_metadata['id3v1']['title'];
        $form['field_album_name'][LANGUAGE_NONE][0]['value']['#default_
           value'] = $file_metadata['id3v1']['album'];
        $form['field_album_year'][LANGUAGE_NONE][0]['value']['#default_
           value'] = $file_metadata['id3v1']['year'];
        $form['field_time'][LANGUAGE_NONE][0]['value']['#default_value']
          = $file_metadata['playtime_string'];


      }
    }
  }
```

This snippet of code is enough for us to hook into the specific form which shows up when a media asset has been uploaded (specifically, an audio file type). At that point, we call the `getid3_analyze()` function, to extract metadata from the uploaded file, using the file object that we observed in the `$form` array. With the metadata array that we extracted, we can then set each of the Drupal audio file type fields that we created before and populate them with their respective metadata information.

There are better ways to structure the module, for example by using the **Features** module and installing these extra metadata fields along with the module, instead of "relying" on these fields hard coded into the module. General error checks are also missing but this is for the sake of code readability.

Because this is a new module that we've created, we need to enable it. Visiting the modules page (`/admin/modules`), we can see our new module listed there, so just toggle it on and click on **Save configuration** to enable the module:

☐	**Store id3**	store_id3 extracts metadata information from media resources and stores them into Drupal fields

Finally, let's remove our own custom Tracks node content type custom template as we don't really need to rely on it anymore, since we will be using the generic node view.

Proceed to clear the cache as we did before to make sure Drupal re-reads the templates directory (`/admin/config/development/performance`).

Now that the module is enabled, proceed to editing an existing audio file entry that you've created before or add a new one. After uploading your audio media file or editing an existing audio media file, the audio field settings form should show up, along with our new metadata fields, which should have their values populated with the information we extracted from the file:

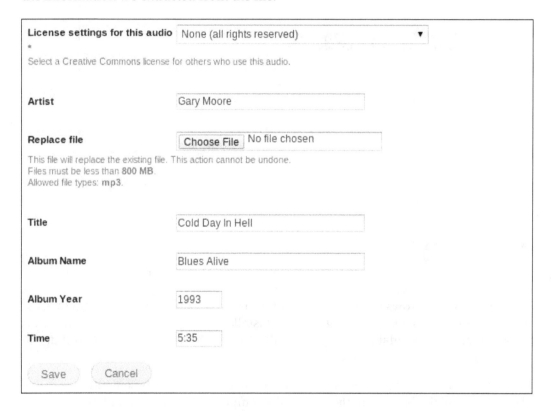

The actual node view is no longer using our customized node template file, so it is expected to show up as earlier with the **MediaElement Audio** widget rendering the audio file, and it's now also displaying the metadata fields that we extracted from the file.

Some ideas to take this forward:

- You might see fit to extract more metadata from the file, and this isn't bound to audio files only—video and image formats may have some interesting data too.

- Create views to list and manage your music collection. With the help of metadata fields you can now filter, search, and sort by each of the fields that you extracted.

Summary

In this chapter, we have covered different ways of working with audio content and learned how to customize audio presentation. We have employed HTML5 technology which browsers support nowadays in favor of allowing audio playback without requiring any special plugins to be installed. Then, we have further utilized the abundance of metadata that is potentially stored in audio media and tied it up with Drupal's content structure.

In the next chapter, we will focus on HTML5 related tools such as semantic HTML and creating visual charts, and further empower our toolbox in Drupal and HTML5 applications.

7
Leveraging Other HTML5 Features

Now that we have acquired knowledge of HTML5, we will look further to see how it can empower Drupal web applications. We will explore more visual eye candy content such as graphs and charting, as well as HTML metadata for interoperability with third-party websites and introduce mobile compatible web layout support.

In this chapter, we will cover:

- More HTML5-related modules to enrich your arsenal for media such as charting and presentation applications
- RDFa and Microdata for more semantic HTML
- The concept of **Responsive Web Design (RWD)**

RDFa and Microdata

One of HTML5's primary goals was to provide a more semantic web, replacing all the <div> and other elements with their class and ID attributes with better-suited elements, such as <article>, <section>, <nav>, and others. In doing that, it was intended to achieve a more semantic document, but what does it mean exactly? In Tim Berners-Lee's own words "the Web will be a place where the whim of a human being and the reasoning of a machine coexist in an ideal, powerful mixture".

This basically means that by creating a more structured web, machines will also be able to understand it and put it into a relative context. Let's identify some real-world examples as follows:

- A pre-HTML5 website might have used the `<input type="text"/>` element to specify a text field for users to provide their phone number. While a desktop user would not mind this, mobile users would find it quite annoying to fill such a field using the full keyboard. Furthermore, on most occasions it requires the developer to also program client-side code to allow only numbers to be typed into this field. With HTML5's `<input type="tel"/>` element, computers are made aware that this is a phone field, which probably only takes numeric values and some special characters and may offer an appropriate popup widget. Even desktop applications such as a program that fills a website's forms automatically can now better understand the purpose of this field and offer better functionality.

- When an HTML page is being indexed by search engines, it's a machine program that scans the text, attempts to make sense out of those bits and pieces, applying all sorts of (machine learning) algorithms to classify that page and categorize it somehow so that it can later be found when you type in a few keywords on a search engine's website.

> The second example brings into context a field in web technology called **Search Engine Optimization (SEO)** which you have probably heard of by now. Some may refer to it as an art which one needs to master, employing a set of skills and knowledge to fine tune the structure of web pages in order to reach the ultimate result in a search engine's indexing algorithms. Drupal out of the box, attempts to optimize as much as possible for this goal, one very obvious method is the use of URL aliases for nodes which create a path of `/content/how-install-drupal` which come a long way in aiding machines classify web pages. As one can expect with Drupal, there are a plenty of other third-party modules in the Drupal eco-system to better fit a website for SEO-friendliness, some of which are the Metatag module (`http://drupal.org/project/metatag`), SEO Checklist, and XML Sitemap.

If semantic mark-up is about describing and providing metadata about the mark-up itself, then how do we achieve this in a more programmatic fashion? With the rise of protocols like **Resource Description Framework in Attributes (RDFa)** and Microdata, this process has become quite streamlined and standardized.

Both RDFa and Microdata make use of vocabularies to describe resources and can make use of locally generated or remotely hosted vocabularies, which are also known as ontologies. The reason for working with such vocabularies is that while one might describe a person using the keyword *person*, another website might define it as *man*, and another as *individual*, all of which mean the same thing. By working with common vocabularies the terms used to describe the meaning of metadata are standardized, and as such, applications can easily interact with one another, as they know what to expect.

Introducing RDFa

RDF in attributes (**RDFa**) is not a new kid on the block. It actually started as RDF almost a decade ago but became a W3C recommendation a few years later, following a first public draft in work.

 RDF serialization is simply a form to represent an RDF data model, much like PHP's own `serialize()` function. While RDFa deals with embedding RDF with XHTML documents, there are other serializations such as RDF/XML, RDF/JSON, and others.

RDF data model makes use of subject, predicate, and object triples to achieve a mapping between metadata and its description, where any metadata can be represented as a resource. An example for such triple is the following pseudo-code:

```
pfx:Me pfx:EmployedBy pfx:Bob
```

Take for example, a news item posted on a news website, for us humans it's very easy to interpret who submitted it, when, and what is this news item about. A stripped-down version of an HTML code for such item might look as follows:

```html
<html>
  <head><title> Breaking news in open source</title></head>
  <body>
    <h1>Oracle Buys Sun</h1>
    <p>Submitted by John Doe … </p>
  </body>
</html>
```

With RDFa and HTML5, the HTML document can be extended with attributes which explain the meaning of each piece of information that is trivial for us humans to understand as follows:

```html
<html
    prefix="dc: http://purl.org/dc/elements/1.1/"
  lang="en">
    <head><title> Breaking news in open source</title></head>
    <body>
    <div
      about="http://example.org/#news">
      Oracle Buys Sun
      <p>Submitted by
        <span property="foaf:name"
          resource="sioc:User"
          about="/user/2600">
          John Doe
        </span>
      </p>
    </div>
  </body>
</html>
```

The HTML document begins with an `<html>` element that contains an additional attribute `prefix`, which includes popular vocabularies like **FOAF (Friend Of A Friend)** and does not require developers to explicitly declare this vocabulary using **XML Namespace (xmlns)** as would be the case when HTML4 is involved. The `<div>` element is also extended with an attribute which expresses the subject in this web page and finally the paragraph element makes use of several other attributes to explain the meaning of the text `John Doe`. The previous RDFa code snippet shows the use of the triples, using the following new attributes that may be applied to HTML elements:

- **about**: It is a URI that expresses what is the metadata about. RDF data model defines this as subject.

- **property**: It is a URI that expresses the relationship between the subject and a metadata. RDF data model defines this as predicate.

- **resource**: It expresses the resource which is associated with the subject, but is not a navigable link rather a text literal link. RDF data model defines this as object.

Existing attributes in XHTML can be used as well, some of which are as follows:

- **typeof**: It indicates the vocabulary language that is used to describe and associate with the subject
- **rel**: It expresses the relationship between two resources, can be often replaced by a property attribute

 RDF was worked on long before HTML5 spec and for this reason its RDFa extension is largely based on the XHTML documents, working with existing attributes as well as introducing new attributes for HTML elements.

You might have noticed the prefixes used in our code example, such as `foaf`, `dc`, and `sioc`. As you can imagine, there are many types of resources that can be described, and therefore many vocabularies that can be used to do so. Some of which that Drupal 7 supports are as follows:

- **dc (Dublin Core)**: This describes generic information about resources such as it's title, time, or date it was created and such.
- **foaf (Friend Of A Friend)**: This vocabulary describes people, their relationships, and their activities.
- **sioc (Semantically Interlinked Online Communities)**: It describes the relationship between collaboration platforms such as blogs and forums. It includes resources like item, post, comment, and number of replies.

Enabling RDF support in Drupal

Drupal 7 ships with RDFa support out of the box and includes default RDF mappings for nodes, comments, taxonomy, and users with support for developers to extend these even further if required. The RDF module may or may not be enabled in your installation of Drupal 7, depending on your deployment, and whether you chose a minimal or standard profile when installing Drupal 7. Whichever the case, let's proceed to enable this module (`/admin/modules`), which doesn't require any configuration.

The core RDF module doesn't provide any administrative configuration pages to tweak the RDF mappings or vocabularies being used. It only offers developers API through which they can create their own settings for node entities and other data structures in Drupal. Due to this limited support of the core RDF module, there's another module that came into the picture, called RDF extensions (`http://drupal.org/project/rdfx`) which offers an administrative UI which allows you to configure specific RDF mappings for nodes and their fields among other features.

Once enabled, we can examine some of the changes introduced by the RDF module to our generated HTML source code by inspecting it using browser tools. Doing so for the Concertz type node for example, we can notice how the `<html>` tag has been extended to include the required prefix which defines the vocabularies it uses as follows:

```
<html lang="en" dir="ltr"
prefix="content: http://purl.org/rss/1.0/modules/content/ dc: http://
purl.org/dc/terms/ foaf: http://xmlns.com/foaf/0.1/ og: http://ogp.
me/ns# rdfs: http://www.w3.org/2000/01/rdf-schema# sioc: http://rdfs.
org/sioc/ns# sioct: http://rdfs.org/sioc/types# skos: http://www.
w3.org/2004/02/skos/core# xsd: http://www.w3.org/2001/XMLSchema#"
class="js"><!--<![endif]--><head>
```

We can easily identify Dublin Core and FOAF which we mentioned earlier, among other vocabularies such as **Simple Knowledge Organization System (SKOS)** available at `http://www.w3.org/TR/skos-reference/`.

Next, we can see how the node mapping to an RDF object shows up in our HTML as follows:

```
<article id="node-16" class="node node-concertz node-promoted
article odd node-full ia-n clearfix"
about="/drupal7/node/16" typeof="sioc:Item foaf:Document"
role="article">
```

The use of the `about` attribute hints the subject of this RDF resource and the `typeof` attribute defines which kind of resource is this using the SIOC and FOAF vocabularies.

And taking a look at the actual node's information such as the title, we can see that it is also now making use of the RDF attributes to explain the meaning of the metadata there:

```
<h1
  property="dc:title"  class="node-title" rel="nofollow">
  Live school show
</h1>
```

That's it! RDFa support provided by Drupal 7 core module is doing all the heavy lifting for us by default. Yet, notice that it relies on the theming system to support it so making use of the widely adopted themes that follow Drupal's guidelines is advised.

> Readers who wish to focus even more on SEO capabilities may look at the Schema.org module (`http://drupal.org/project/schemaorg`) which provides integration with `http://www.schema.org` as its vocabulary. Google, Bing, Yahoo!, and others are known to understand and rely on `schema.org` structure which would probably yield in better results than the core RDFa module, such as Google's rich snippets in search engine results.

Introducing Microdata

While W3C has released an official specification RDFa 1.1 support in HTML5 (`http://dev.w3.org/html5/rdfa`), Microdata (`http://www.whatwg.org/specs/web-apps/current-work/multipage/microdata.html`) was initially developed as part of the HTML5 design spec. Based on the roots of RDFa, it aims to provide a semantic web by annotating elements in a more simplified manner. It is also the recommended data mark-up structure by Google to enhance search results using Google Rich Snippets (`http://support.google.com/webmasters/bin/answer.py?hl=en&answer=99170`) as shown in the following screenshot:

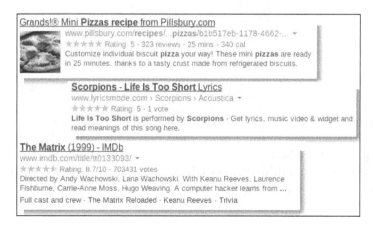

Microdata makes use of attributes for items and their properties. For example, a recipe is an item which has properties, like the time it takes to make the dish. Whereas properties are commonly set to use text literals (text strings), they can also describe another item. For example, the author of a recipe is a property which describes another item—the actual person.

In Microdata syntax we use the attribute `itemprop` to set item properties and the `itemscope` attribute to put the properties into context or so called containers, so that parsers know for which item those properties are set for. To further allow machines which parse this data to understand what kind of item is this, the use of the `itemtype` attribute is employed.

Enabling Microdata support in Drupal

To take this into a more practical approach, let's see how we can improve our HTML pages to be more semantic, and describe it better to bots such as search engine crawlers. For the Microdata protocol we will work with our recipes content type, but first we will need to download and enable the Microdata module (`http://drupal.org/project/microdata`) for Drupal.

Once we have decided upon the content type we will need to make sure that there is an appropriate vocabulary for this item type. In our example, the quite standard vocabulary at `schema.org` features a recipe item at `http://schema.org/Recipe` and by examining its support for item properties we can see that it supports some of the fields that we already added to our content type:

Properties from Recipe		
cookingMethod	Text	The method of cooking, such as Frying, Steaming, ...
cookTime	Duration	The time it takes to actually cook the dish, in ISO 8601 duration format.
ingredients	Text	An ingredient used in the recipe.
nutrition	NutritionInformation	Nutrition information about the recipe.
prepTime	Duration	The length of time it takes to prepare the recipe, in ISO 8601 duration format.
recipeCategory	Text	The category of the recipe—for example, appetizer, entree, etc.
recipeCuisine	Text	The cuisine of the recipe (for example, French or Ethopian).
recipeInstructions	Text	The steps to make the dish.
recipeYield	Text	The quantity produced by the recipe (for example, number of people served, number of servings, etc).
totalTime	Duration	The total time it takes to prepare and cook the recipe, in ISO 8601 duration format.

Now that we have obtained this knowledge, we can proceed to configure our rezepi content type and make use of this information. Navigate to **Structure | Content types | rezepi | edit** (`/admin/structure/types/manage/rezepi`) where you should see the newly added Microdata settings field-set and notice that each setting description text is quite helpful here as shown in the following screenshot:

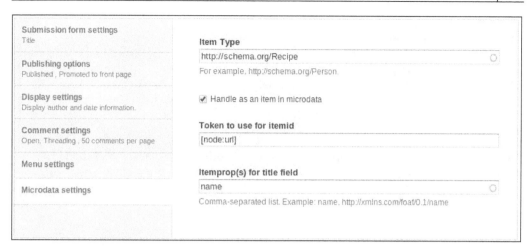

We have already identified the **item type** so we know to set it to `http://schema.org/Recipe`. The use of tokens is very handy here as it replaces the `[node:url]` string with the URL for each node with its actual URL which gets set as the item type. And lastly the properties to set for this item type for which we chose simply the **name** property, the value of which will be the name of each node's recipe.

So far we have only configured the item type, we still have to configure the properties for it, which are identified as our fields for this content type in Drupal's terms. To do so, navigate to the **MANAGE FIELDS** tab of the rezepi content type (`/admin/structure/types/manage/rezepi/fields`) and edit the **Cuisine** field type which maps to **recipeCuisine** item property on `schema.org`. Scrolling to the very end of the field's configuration page we can see this setting added by the Microdata module and we'll set it appropriately as shown in the following screenshot:

You are encouraged to go ahead and setup more fields, at the very least, the basic elements such as description, image, and the rest of the supported text fields.

Ideally, one should take efforts to configure every content type's fields as much as possible to provide the best interoperability, as well as SEO compatibility. With that said, some fields such as dates, should be annotated in a very specific format which schema.org demands. This means that field formatters or the Microdata module itself should provide support for identifying such cases.

Now that our item and it's properties have been defined we can inspect the HTML source code for a rezepi content that was added earlier. Paying a close attention, we can see that both the item type, as well as its **Cuisine** property, are showing up.

The **Cuisine** item property is as follows:

```
<section class="field field-name-field-cuisine field-type-
list-text field-label-above view-mode-full"><h2 class="field-
label">Cuisine: </h2><div class="field-items" id="md15"><div
class="field-item even" itemprop="recipeCuisine">Iraqi</div></div></
section>
```

The **Recipe** content type is as follows:

```
<div>
    <meta  itemscope="" itemtype="http://schema.org/Recipe"
      itemid="http://sites-dev.hp.com/drupal7/node/3"
    temref="md1 md3 md5 md7 md9 md11 md13 md14 md15 md16 md17 md18
      md19 md20" />
    <meta  itemscope="" itemref="md21" /><meta  itemscope=""
      itemprop="ingredients" id="md3" itemref="md2" />
    <meta  itemscope="" itemprop="ingredients" id="md5"
      itemref="md4" />
    <meta  itemscope="" itemprop="ingredients" id="md7"
      itemref="md6" />
    <meta  itemscope="" itemprop="ingredients" id="md9"
      itemref="md8" />
    <meta  itemscope="" itemprop="ingredients" id="md11"
      itemref="md10" />
    <meta  itemscope="" itemprop="ingredients" id="md13"
      itemref="md12" />
</div>
```

Testing semantic mark-up

To accommodate the embedding of semantic mark-up for web builders, more than a few tools and online web services have been made available to test and provide feedback, as well as visualization, of semantic HTML.

For Microdata, some of these tools are as follows:

- Microdata JS (`http://gitorious.org/microdatajs` which hosts an online tool to test live sites called Live Microdata ;`http://foolip.org/microdatajs/live`)
- SEO Moves (`http://tools.seomoves.org/microdata`)

And for RDFa one can try out `http://rdfa.info/play/`. Even Google has an online service at `http://www.google.com/webmasters/tools/richsnippets` which provides a lot of feedback for site builders, displaying how data is being parsed out of your HTML source code, including displaying a sample search results for the purpose of rich snippets.

Since we have been working on our Microdata recipe item, let's see how machines, which parse our HTML source code, attempt to understand it. I've made use of the Live Microdata tool (`http://gitorious.org/microdatajs`) which enables you to copy-and-paste the HTML code and parse it:

```
Preview    JSON    vCard    iCal

{
  "items": [
    {
      "type": [
        "http://schema.org/Recipe"
      ],
      "id": "http://sites-dev.hp.com/drupal7/node/3",
      "properties": {
        "name": [
          "Kubbeh Soup"
        ],
        "recipeCategory": [
          "Main Dish"
        ],
        "recipeCuisine": [
          "Iraqi"
        ],
        "cookTime": [
          "1180180 minutes"
        ],
        "ingredients": [
          {
            "properties": {}
          },
          {
            "properties": {}
          },
          {
            "properties": {}
          },
          {
            "properties": {}
          },
          {
            "properties": {}
          },
          {
            "properties": {}
          }
        ]
      }
    },
    {
      "properties": {}
    }
  ]
}
```

Visualizing data with graphical charts

These days, more than ever, the web is making use of graphical charts to visualize data. Tools which provide information about trends, analytics and statistics have been made available for users to leverage insights.

The rise of big data technology (http://en.wikipedia.org/wiki/Big_data) enables computers to perform complex analysis and produce insights on large scale data. With the help of smart algorithms, information can be visualized in a simple manner using graphical charts. Evidence to this can be see in Google's Trends tool (http://www.google.com/trends), and other services such as Google Analytics or Google Adsense. YouTube's video statistics are a common use and even SoundCloud, where a user can take a look at his or hers audio tracks popularity trend as shown in the following screenshot:

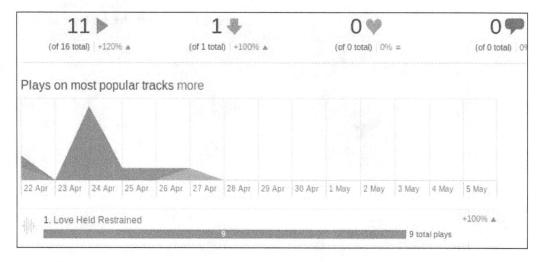

Versions prior to Drupal 7 featured charting modules based on open source libraries, such as open flash charts which required browser's Adobe Flash plug-in support to render the charts. Other, non-Flash solutions existed, and still do today, such as Google's Chart API (which was deprecated a while ago in benefit of a newer version) on-top of other open source libraries but those were mostly based on creating JavaScript or image-based charts. The problem with such solutions is that images won't be interactive, and won't be supported well on mobile devices.

Scalable Vector Graphics, also known as SVG, has been adopted by HTML5 and forms a key part in the spec, for the purpose of providing two-dimensional vector or raster graphics. Due to its vector nature, SVG is resolution independent which basically means that the same image will look good on any screen size, whether it's a desktop or a mobile device.

SVG is actually a language that is expressed by XML in order to create an image and is well supported by popular tools such as Inkscape, Illustrator, and browsers are able to render them easily. Vector graphics can be mixed with raster images such as PNG and JPG as well as text and even create animations and provide user interactivity. Moreover, because bandwidth consideration is crucial for solid web performance, SVG makes a great adoption for HTML5, because it can be entirely built by simply creating XML documents and even compressed by the popular GZIP protocol for transfer over the wire.

With modern browser's support for HTML5 we can make use of the SVG images to provide graphical visualization for charts. While there are many options to use, a popular charting solution is Google's new Chart Tools API (`https://developers.google.com/chart`) which provides a JavaScript interface for web builders to implement and create charts as shown in the following screenshot:

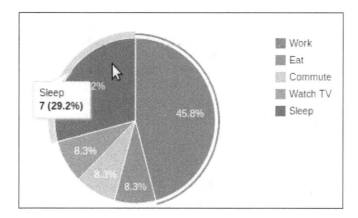

 We chose Google Chart Tools API as it is a mature and established product that is used both internally and by other third-party developers. The API offers support for many types of charts among the popular column (commonly known as bar charts) and line charts. For example, you can create geo charts which make use of visual maps, as well as animated gauges.

Enabling charts in Drupal

Our module of choice is Visualization API (`http://drupal.org/project/visualization`) which has been adopted by another module called Commerce Reporting (`http://drupal.org/project/commerce_reports`) and makes a good customer reference to observe the charting capabilities made possible.

For the Visualization API module, proceed to download the 7.x-1.x-dev release, which to this date only contains documentation updates, but we're going to make use of its API later, so it's a good decision to go with. Once downloaded and enabled we only need to configure the charting library API of choice. Navigate to **Configuration | System | Visualization** (`/admin/config/system/visualization`) and make sure **Preferred charting library** is set to **Google Visualization API** and click on **Save configuration**.

You may find another charting module useful, based on SVG and the JavaScript library `Raphael.js` (`https://drupal.org/project/raphael`).

Although open source charting solutions exist, such as Google's Chart Tools API, organization may wish to use commercial products to host the code locally, to benefit from developer support channel, or other reasons. One popular option in this case is Highcharts (`http://www.highcharts.com/`) which is a well-established library and is also supported by our choice of Drupal's Visualization API module.

The module supports both a developer's API for programmatically creating charts as well as built-in Views support to render charts easily using the UI and nothing but the Views module. We will investigate both options at hand, starting with the Views UI.

Visualization API using Views

Building a view requires some planning, with regards to what fields we need to pull in from the database. To begin with, we should ask ourselves, what are we trying to graph and whether there's a way to get this information from views? In most cases, charts create graphs out of numeric data.

To work with our existing content types, we can make use of the **Cooking Time** field for the rezepi content type to show a trend graph for submitted recipes and their cooking time. With this in mind we may proceed to create this chart using views.

Navigate to **Structure | Views | Add new view** (/admin/structure/views/
add) and let's begin with naming the view; **Cooking Time Trend** seems to nail it.
Set the same value for the **Page Title** too and update the **Display format** to use
Visualization of type **fields** and click on **Continue & edit**.

In the created view settings we need to make use of the fields which will make our
x and y axis. The x axis will show each recipe's name and the y axis will show the
cooking time for it.

Back to the view's page display, the content node's title field is already showing up
by default in the **FIELDS** section as **Content:Title**. Click on the **add** button and locate
the **Content: Cooking Time** field to add and click on **Apply**. The default settings for
this field serve us well, so click on **Apply (all displays)** to finish. To make sure we're
only querying rezepi content type click on the **add** button in the **FILTER CRITERIA**
section and toggle on the **Content: Type** filter type.

To set the actual visualization related configuration click on **Settings** for the **Format
Visualization** section and a configuration pop-up window will display. Our
previous planning regarding the x and y axis as well as specifying the chart type
happens in this form. We will use the **Line chart** option for **Chart type** and enable
the **FIELD_COOKING_TIME** option with the **X-axis labels** set to **Content: Title**
and **Y-axis** title set to **Cooking time**. The result should look the following screenshot:

To further enhance our Cooking Time Trend chart let's also add filters to it and expose them to the user to manipulate. We can do this with no considerable effort as the view module creates the query for us.

In the **FILTER CRITERIA** section click on the **add** button and search for **Content: Post date**, toggle it on and click on **Apply (all displays)**. For its **operators** setting, use the **is between** option and toggle on the option **Expose this filter to visitors, to allow them to change it**, and finally click on **Apply (all displays)** once more to save the field settings.

The final configuration for the Cooking Time Trend chart view should look like the following screenshot:

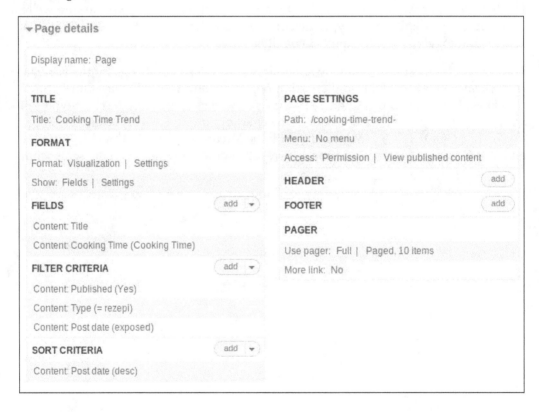

We're done with the view settings. Make sure you don't forget to click on **Save** now at the top right. To view the results of the chart that we created click on the **view page** button or if you've followed our naming convention for this view, simply navigate to /cooking-time-trend.

As you can see, we created a stand-alone page using the Views module UI that displays an interactive chart which also supports user exposed filters as shown in the following screenshot:

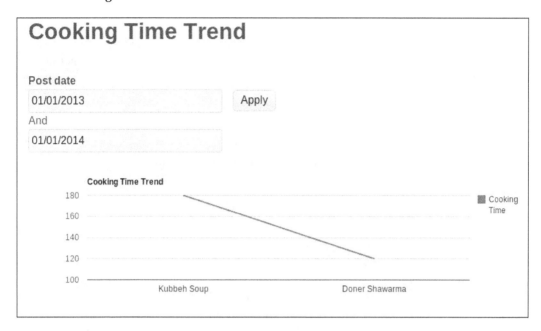

The integration of the Visualization API's module with the Views module is not limited to only one chart per page. One can also create such views and define them as blocks and then place them anywhere on the page which the theme's defined regions allow. One can further more make use of more than one view by programmatically calling views from code.

Visualization API developer interface

While Visualization API module has decent integration with the Views module, for most analytics metrics that you'd be interested in pulling out of your Drupal site, you might find that you really want that freedom to create your own database calls and a very specific SQL query to yield the data out.

Let's make use of the module's developer API to create a chart that will show us as site builders, the content creation trend on a daily basis. With the help of this analysis, we will get insights regarding the busier days of the week where content gets created. Moreover, we will use Drupal's blocks system to declare this chart as a block, which will then allow us the freedom to display it wherever we want in the theme's regions.

Starting out with building our new module for this chart, we will need to create the module's directory and two essential files for the module: the `.info` file and the `.module` file. I've named the module `packtpub_charts` which maps to the following directory and files structure:

- `sites/all/modules/packtpub_charts` as the module directory
- `sites/all/modules/packtpub_charts/packtpub_charts.info` as the module's metadata information file
- `sites/all/modules/packtpub_charts/packtpub_charts.module` as the module's code file

Once you have created the previously mentioned files structure we will begin with creating the `.info` file for the module and adding the following contents to it:

```
name = PacktPub Charts
description = Example module to create charts using the Visualization
API
core = 7.x
dependencies[] = visualization
```

As we mentioned before, when building custom modules through-out this chapter, this file is used as a general information, which Drupal counts on to figure out which version is the module for, what its name, and whether it depends on other modules or not. As we can clearly see there's a `dependencies[]` directive set which informs Drupal that this module depends on the Visualization API module. Moving on to the `.module` file we will begin with implementing Drupal's block hooks which will create the block entry for us and define a callback function which creates the charts as the content of the block as follows:

```php
<?php

/**
 * Implements hook_block_info().
 *
 */
function packtpub_charts_block_info() {
  $blocks['content_creation_trend'] = array(
    'info' => t('Chart: Content Creation Trend'),
    'cache' => DRUPAL_NO_CACHE,
  );

  return $blocks;
}
```

```
/**
 * Implements hook_block_view().
 *
 */
function packtpub_charts_block_view($delta = '') {
  $block = array();

  switch ($delta) {
    case 'content_creation_trend':
      $block['subject'] = t('Content Creation Trend');
      /* Define a callback function which will return an array that
         Drupal uses to figure out how to render the content for
         this block */
      $block['content'] = packtpub_charts_chart_content_creation_
        trend();
      break;
  }
  return $block;
}
```

Finally, moving on to the more interesting part of our chart module, our callback function which create the charts. Visualization API developer interface expects to receive its data points as a hashed array with labels and their values. For example, if we wanted to create a chart for weather in some countries (specified in Celsius metric) we would use the following code:

```
$data = array(
  array('country' => 'Israel', 'weather' => 26),
  array('country' => 'Barcelona', 'weather' => 15),
  array('country' => 'Cluj', 'weather' => 3),
);
```

That code creates a dataset array which holds other arrays of points. Each point array is composed of a `country` key which indicates the country label as well as a `weather` key which indicates the value for each country.

In reality, you would almost never have such hard-coded data points but would rather need to get this information from a data-store (like a database) or maybe by querying a RESTful service. In our case, we will need to query the database to return information about the number of nodes that were created in each day of the week.

The following code snippet shows callback which creates the chart, let's examine the code first and explain the flow afterwards:

```
/**
 * Callback to create chart data array for content creation trend
 *
 */
function packtpub_charts_chart_content_creation_trend() {

  $sql = "SELECT COUNT( n.nid ) AS count, DATE_FORMAT(
    FROM_UNIXTIME( n.created ) ,  '%a' ) AS day FROM
  {node} n GROUP BY day";
  $result = db_query($sql);

  $data = array();
  foreach ($result as $item) {
    $nodes = array();
    $nodes['day'] = $item->day;
    $nodes['count'] = $item->count;
    $data[] = $nodes;
  }

  $chart = array(
    'title' => t('Content Creation Trend'),
    'fields' => array(
      'count' => array(
        'label' => t('Count'),
        'enabled' => TRUE,
      ),
    'day' => array(
      'label' => t('Day'),
      'enabled' => TRUE,
    ),
  ),
  'xAxis' => array(
    'labelField' => 'day',
    ),
  'data' => $data,
  'type' => 'pie',
);

  return array(
    '#theme' => 'visualization',
    '#options' => $chart,
    );
}
```

The code does the following:

- Defines the query to pull the information from the database. As you can see, the query already organizes the counts and days in a key=value type of resultset. Because the node table defines a created field in Unix timestamp we make use of MySQL's `data_format()` and `from_unixtime()` functions to convert this data to MySQL's date/time notation and format it to return the text literal for day of the week.

- The `foreach()` statement loops through the resultset values and creates the array data points such as in our country weather example.

- The `$chart` associative array defines the following charts properties:
    - **title**: It sets the title for the chart as a string
    - **fields**: It is an associative array which defines the fields for the chart. `xaxis` – sets the field to be used on the X axis, which is each day. Y-axis will show the actual counts.
    - **data**: It sets the data points array wrapper that we created through the `foreach()` loop that is, `$data`
    - **type**: It sets the type of the chart, which as you can see, this chart will be rendered as pie

- As the last step, we return an associative array where the `#theme` key tells Drupal to format this data with the Visualization API's module `visualization` theme and the `#options` key passes it our data to render.

The module is now finished and we need to enable it first and then navigate to the blocks administration page (`/admin/structure/blocks`), locate the block called **Chart: Content Creation Trend** and set it to one of the theme's regions. Once you refresh the front page or another Drupal page (depending on the theme region you picked up) you should see the following chart in the screenshot show up as a block:

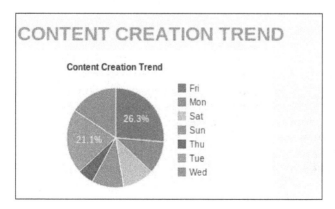

If you'd like to experiment with things, try to simply change the pie type in the `$chart` array code to say `column`. Now that you've obtained the skills to create your own charts from Drupal's database nothing stops you from realizing your own unique ideas for site analytics.

Responsive web design

In responsive design, a web layout design implements a theme or template structure which adapts to the browser's viewport width and resolution. For example, consider a website which has several horizontal columns and possibly a horizontal menu too. Loading this website on a mobile smartphone would require the device's browser to zoom out completely to render the page and force the user to excessively scroll up and down, left and right to navigate through the website. Instead, if the website could somehow detect that it's been viewed by a mobile device and even detect it's measures (height and width) it could then take action to render the HTML differently so it would create just a single column of content as shown in the following screenshot:

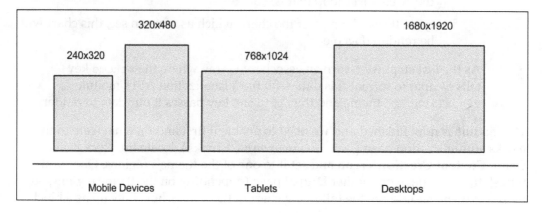

Adaptive Web Design (AWD) versus Responsive Web Design (RWD)

With the AWD approach, a web builder prepares several page template layouts before-hand to fit a specific device's resolution which when detected the web application uses the relevant page template. With the RWD approach, a web builder makes use of a fluid grid system for the layout, where using CSS programming techniques (such as media queries which we will talk about shortly) the browser makes changes to the layout when the screen resolution changes.

Taking `http://mashable.com` as an example, this website renders along the lines of the following screenshot if you view it from a desktop (or at least a large enough resolution to get the three column layout):

Surfing the same website from a mobile devices with a relatively smaller screen size (320 pixel resolution and even up to 480 pixels) it will render as follows:

It's not just about mobile devices but also about adapting the layout for the current screen resolution. You can try this out easily by resizing your browser size gradually and seeing the layout change on the fly.

The frontend development arena has been stirring quite a lot of noise in the recent years. Whether it's responsive web design, semantic web, HTML5, or node.js, the buzz-words keep piling up with technology and mobile devices in particular, re-inventing themselves year over year.

To put some order in all of this, let's define some basic terms as follows:

- **Mobile First**: Smartphones, tablets, and other types of hybrid mobile devices pose a priority in terms of web design strategy, where planning of a given web application begins with those devices in mind and consider their support to render the application as a viewable item. This is opposed to the quite familiar method of designing a web application for desktop browsers while providing some graceful degradation for some unsupported features and reduced viewport size.

- **Feature Detection**: In the beginning we had browser detection, an old detection method where servers attempt to detect which browser is in use based on the USER_AGENT HTTP header. Due to many reasons (such as unreliable header that may be faked as well as others), this evolved into feature detection which attempts to detect which capabilities the browser support, such as HTML5 or even CSS features. Using this information, the server can respond with a web layout which fits best the client's browser.

- **Media Queries**: These are part of the CSS3 specification and enable website builders to customize the content rendering based on the device's features. For example, if a device's resolution has been detected to be smaller than 760x480, then it will apply a different style to some CSS class. It can also provide a completely different CSS file based on the resolution. Media queries may help detect different device features such as width, height, orientation (landscape or portrait on mobile devices), and others.

Responsive web design with AdaptiveTheme

While there are many themes available in the Drupal eco-system, primarily the leading options Omega and Zen, a user can easily get lost while choosing the right option. yet the AdaptiveTheme project is one of the options at the top of that list. It offers quite a bit of integration with popular modules such as Panels and Display Suite. Its rapidly evolving feature set and framework foundation enable developers to re-use its powerful responsive design methods and cross-browser support to build on.

AdaptiveTheme (`http://drupal.org/project/adaptivetheme`) is bundled with three themes. The AT Core and AT Subtheme which act as a theme package and enable developers to extend a skeleton and build upon. It also features the at_admin package which may serve as an administrative theme. To accommodate for a proper sub theme we made use of Corolla (`http://drupal.org/project/corolla`) but there are other supported subthemes available, namely AT Commerce (`http://drupal.org/project/at-commerce`) for e-commerce web applications and provides complete integration with the Commerce module (`http://drupal.org/project/commerce`).

 When choosing sub themes, make sure that their minor versions match. If you're going to use AdaptiveTheme 7.x-3.x make sure you also use the 7.x-3.x Version of the sub theme you choose.

Before we move on with the theme's configuration, let's first spread our blocks across the possible regions to make sure that we are using both sidebars. To do this, navigate to **Structure | Blocks** (`/admin/structure/block`) and set some of the blocks to use the **Sidebar first** region and others to use **Sidebar second** region. Once you're done click on the **Save blocks** button and visit the frontpage to make sure that the layout is composed of three columns where one of them is the main content.

To access the Corolla theme configuration page navigate to **Appearance** and click on the **Settings** link next to the Corolla theme logo (`/admin/appearance/settings/corolla`). As you can see the theme is abundant of configuration options, from page responsive layout, to different extensions like fonts, and image styling.

The responsive layout that the theme provides is broken up across three main categories, **Standard Layout**, **Tablet Layout**, and **Smartphone Layout**. Each of these layouts kick-in, depending on the detected resolution (using media queries) and defines the layout properties, such as how many columns and their positions (even allowing to configure each column's width length):

- **Standard Layout**: Basically any desktop-like workstation including laptops and stationary screens which can't tilt and usually have high resolution
- **Tablet** and **Smartphone Layout**: They are relevant for mobile devices and further enable layout configuration based on the orientation of the device (portrait or landscape)

Now that we understand this setup, let's configure it so that when viewing our website from any resolution above 2000px (mine is set at 1920x1080 but if you're screen is using a higher resolution than pick a larger resolution threshold to use) it will use the **Standard Layout** and configure the tablet's layout to kick in for resolutions within the scope of our screen. This way we will force one of the mobile layouts to kick in (specifically the **Tablet Layout**).

To achieve this, go to **Standard Layout** and set the configuration option **Media query for this layout *** to a value of **only screen and (min-width:2000px)**. Then go to **Tablet Layout** and set the same configuration option to the value of **only screen and (min-width:769px) and (max-width:1999px)** (once again, adjust the 1999px to the maximum + 1 resolution of your screen). In the **Tablet Layout** you can also toggle on one of the other layouts than the default, for example the third option which sets one sidebar at the left and the other one at the bottom of the page.

Next, we can turn on some debugging to help us figure out screen sizes. Click on the **Debuggers** vertical tab option in the **Layout & General Settings** configuration area. The **Highlight regions** option will simply highlight the available block regions when viewing a page, much like the blocks administration screen can do. Toggle on the second option, which will let you know of the detected screen size when viewing a page — **Show window size - appears in the bottom right corner**.

Web developers often find browser plugins to be a much helpful tool to ease their life. While you probably know of the popular Firebug tool, there are tools which come in handy for responsive web design, one of which is called Window Resizer that you can search for in Chrome's web store or make use of Firesizer for Firefox (`https://addons.mozilla.org/en-US/firefox/addon/firesizer`). It's a small extension that allows you to resize your browser window to different (standard) sizes with a click of a button and it also notifies you upon resizing a browser window screen which resolution are you on.

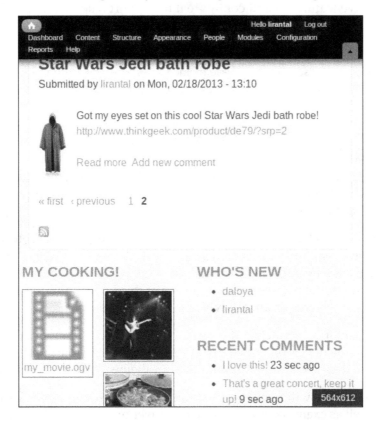

In the same configuration area we can also note the supported layouts and clearly see the list of media queries which the theme bundles with — a total of five configurable layouts out of the box.

Click on **Save configuration** at the bottom on the screen and navigate to the front page and see how responsive design looks now, adopting the layout which we have configured to your screen size. If you try to further resize the browser to match a screen resolution of a smartphone, you should get the following result:

When looking at this page in that resolution you can notice several things:

- The horizontal menu at the top of the page has changed to make it fit the entire screen width so that you wouldn't have to scroll left and right.
- The content column has resized to the entire screen width so that all elements show up.

- The two sidebars that we have assigned blocks for are using the tablet portrait layout where the two columns are both stacked at the bottom of the page, one next to the other. This layout is defined by the media query only screen and (minimum width:481px) and (maximum width:768px) which is in the range of the browser's screen size as we can see in the bottom right tool-tip.

By choosing the correct and appropriate theme for our use, we were able to benefit from its extensive feature set and configure it to support responsive web design so that our web application renders well on mobile devices too.

 You may also consider a base theme that is based on Twitter Bootstrap framework `https://drupal.org/project/bootstrap`.

Summary

By enabling RDF support in our Drupal's website we've made sure that it connects better with other websites, allowing for better interoperability as well as SEO-optimized state of our website.

We have then explored a more visual world of enabling graphical charts with the help of the Views user interface as well as our own custom code where we can tie-in any reports we want by querying the database directly. To make sure these charts render on any modern browser without the use of third-party plugins as well as on mobile devices we leveraged an API which is HTML5-based.

To close this chapter we scratched the surface of advanced theming in the vast world of client-side development where HTML5 plays a key role and learned about responsive web design and how to configure our theme to accommodate this need.

In the next chapter we will further explore image configuration which Drupal provides, as well as examine more tools to empower media content such as enabling a rating mechanism as is very common amongst social networks, and provide better user experience for our users.

8
Enhancing Media Content

In this chapter we will be revisiting some media resources such as images and videos, and enriching the user experience when handling these types of media assets. We will familiarize ourselves better with a site builder's ability to influence the underlying configuration and fine-tune settings relating to media resources.

In this chapter, we will:

- Understand the components of media assets and their configuration
- Leverage the Colorbox module to enhance the user's experience with images
- Use the Plupload integration module to enable multiple file uploads simultaneously
- Understand the use of image styles, extending them with third-party modules for enabling more image effects, as well as with custom module code
- Introduce the Fivestar module as a means of rating content and allowing users to provide feedback on content

Understanding media configuration

Until now we have navigated through a Drupal website across many configuration pages and settings. In this chapter, we will further elaborate on the key areas which make up the media configuration for a Drupal site.

The media related plugins that we've installed on our site, as well as Drupal's own handling for media and files in general, offer configuration settings so that site builders can modify them to meet their needs. We will review these settings and examine particularly those which are relevant to how media assets are handled.

The filesystem

The filesystem configuration, which can be found by navigating to **Configuration | Media | File System** (`/admin/config/media/file-system`), allows us to tune the directory paths where files will be stored when uploaded to Drupal, regardless of whether they are uploaded via Drupal's image widget or the Media module's media library upload widget.

When working with a public filesystem path, files are placed in a directory accessible over the Web, for example, `http://example.com/files/picture.png` (you might have seen URLs in the form `/files/styles/public/picture.png`, which we will elaborate on later). In this case, requests for files are being served directly by the web server and do not go through Drupal's permission and node access mechanism, directly rendering them public to the world.

While the public filesystem may be good for starting out with Drupal to build your site, there are probably good chances you will eventually have to move to a private filesystem due to security reasons. For example, enabling your users to upload their recipes and pictures of themselves will be appealing to members of your website, but this might not be the case if they can't control the visibility of these pictures to only allow their friends, who are members on your site, to view them. When the private filesystem is used, the directory path that you should provide exists outside of Drupal's root directory (the directory where the main `index.php` file is located), yet the web server needs read and write permissions to that directory. With the private filesystem, Drupal creates a placeholder URL that maps to the actual uploaded file in the filesystem, thus providing access control capabilities to such private files.

> A typical configuration of PHP usually allows up to a couple of megabytes of file uploads. To set a larger file size limit you will need to set `upload_max_filesize` and `post_max_size`, which are the directives of `php.ini`.

Image toolkit

Drupal integrates with an image manipulation library to enable tuning of images that are being uploaded to your site. Most probably, you will have the GD Graphics Library installed and available for Drupal to use this functionality exposed through PHP. Otherwise it's possible to install the ImageMagick tool to provide this functionality.

Once an image manipulation tool is integrated, Drupal by default uses it to set the quality of uploaded pictures. To inspect or modify this setting navigate to **Configuration** | **Media** | **Image toolkit** (`/admin/config/media/image-toolkit`).

The importance of the image toolkit functionality is not just about setting the JPEG quality, but also introduces support for abstracting the way images are manipulated so that a rule can be created, for example, to resize all uploaded images automatically to a certain resolution.

Image styles

Image styles are used to create presets of images, defining properties such as sizes (by resizing or scaling up/down), as well as applying other types of image effects. Image styles help a site builder by defining a profile which can be used to format the display of several fields, so when you need to change image properties, you can change the image style, and it will affect all fields that are using it. This is often referred to as weak coupling in software development and it's a good thing because it creates more "freedom" across all moving parts.

There is no need to worry about the changes made to images uploaded to the site. The styles are applied to a copy of the image, for each relevant style, and are saved in the filesystem, along with the original image that was uploaded. Upon changing the properties of an image style, all existing instances that use this image style will be recreated according to the new style settings.

 Image styles pictures are saved to the filesystem using a particular directory structure which you can easily spot, such as `/sites/default/files/styles/thumbnail/public/picture.png`.

In previous Drupal versions this functionality has been provided using modules such as ImageCache, but in Drupal 7 it is already built-in and provides three default styles: thumbnail, medium, and large.

To manage image styles we'll navigate to **Configuration | Media | Image styles** (`/admin/config/media/image-styles`) and we will notice a few styles, that the Media Gallery module added, as well as the options to edit them or add new styles.

Image styles ⊕

Home » Administration » Configuration » Media

Image styles commonly provide thumbnail sizes by scaling and cropping images, but can also add various effects before an image is displayed. When an image is displayed with a style, a new file is created and the original image is left unchanged.

✛ Add style

STYLE NAME	SETTINGS	OPERATIONS
thumbnail	Default	edit
medium	Default	edit
large	Default	edit
square_thumbnail	Default	edit
media_gallery_thumbnail	Default	edit
media_gallery_large	Default	edit

We will add a new thumbnail image style that has a few properties such as scaling, resizing, and color effect to make it black and white. To make sure we understand this style when we use it in other places we will name it `grayscale_thumbnail`.

Click on **Add style** (`/admin/config/media/image-styles/add`), set the new image style name to `grayscale_thumbnail`, and click on **Create new style**, which redirects us to the new image style configuration page. The top of this page is split into two panes, the left side showing how an original image would look like, and on the right side it shows a preview example for our new image style, according to the image effects that we added.

In the **EFFECT** configuration choose the **Scale** effect and click on the **Add** button. Configure the sizes you see fit for a thumbnail picture and click on **Add effect** when done. Then choose the **Desaturate** effect and click on **Add**.

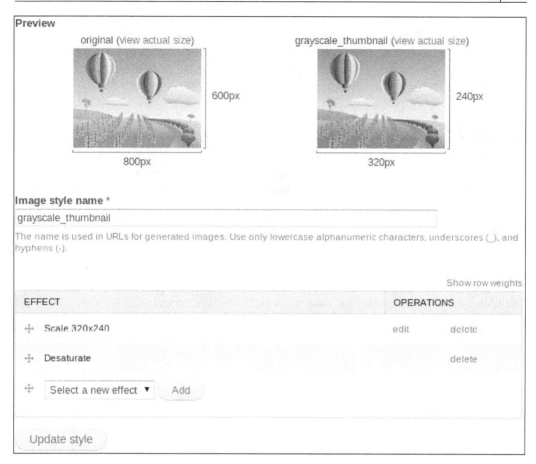

After creating this new image style, we will assign it to one of the content types we created earlier that is using an Image field. This feature should sound familiar as we've used image styles in the beginning, with our Memo content type, where we managed the field's display and chose an image style for one of the Image fields. An image style may be used across our website for different implementations, whether it's galleries, node display modes, views, and so on.

As you can see, the **Image Styles** configuration bundles has three default styles: thumbnail, medium, and large, to accommodate for most scenarios. There are also some built-in effects such as resizing and cropping. We will later on learn how to extend these image styles.

Colorbox

We have made use of the colorbox library earlier to create a pop-up effect for pictures. This was mostly focused on galleries, but we will now learn how to integrate this feature with other parts of a Drupal website.

Colorbox for media images

When we explored the galleries and slideshows functionality before, we made use of Drupal modules which had the sole purpose of meeting that specific requirement. While we were able to meet our functionality of creating galleries, content items that we created did not benefit from the gallery pop-up view, which we later implemented with the help of jQuery's lightbox module.

To remember what this actually means, let's navigate to one of the earlier content types we created, **rezepi**, and take a look at how a node looked like back then. Taking as an example the Kubbeh Soup content item we added, you can clearly see that the images showing up are just as static picture contents.

By enabling the colorbox functionality for plain images too, we can also better style our content nodes by displaying thumbnail pictures which take less screen real-estate, and when users click on them they open up in the lightbox pop up that we've seen previously with the Media Gallery module.

To begin, we will need to add the Colorbox Drupal integration module. Download the latest 7.x stable version (`http://drupal.org/project/colorbox`) and as usual install and enable the module. The Colorbox module introduces many settings to customize the lightbox effect, so we will proceed to its configuration page by navigating to **Configuration** | **Media** | **Images** (`/admin/config/media/colorbox`).

Toggling on the **EXTRA FEATURES** options will provide the integration for the colorbox library and allow leveraging this functionality across your site for other modules too. These options should probably be toggled on by default, if they aren't, it's a good idea to do so.

EXTRA FEATURES

☑ Enable Colorbox load

This enables custom links that can open forms and paths in a Colorbox. Add the class "colorbox-load" to the link and build the url like this for forms "/colorbox/form/[form_id]?destination=some_path&width=500&height=500" and like this for paths "[path]?width=500&height=500&iframe=true" or "[path]?width=500&height=500" if you don't want an iframe. Other modules may activate this for easy Colorbox integration.

☑ Enable Colorbox inline

This enables custom links that can open inline content in a Colorbox. Add the class "colorbox-inline" to the link and build the url like this "?width=500&height=500&inline=true#id-of-content". Other modules may activate this for easy Colorbox integration.

In the **STYLES AND OPTIONS** section we are able to customize the look and feel of the lightbox that pops up. Some styles are available by default yet we can extend them for our specific theme's layout if required. While the **Options** checkbox is set to **Default**, you can toggle on the **Custom** option and notice the very detailed level to which the lightbox popup can be further customized, whether it's the transition effect, its speed, its alpha level, and so on.

The **ADVANCED SETTINGS** section allows for more fine-tuning of the lightbox behavior, for example disabling it on some pages, such as on the admin and node editing pages by default and whether to minify the lightbox's library JavaScript code. The defaults here are most probably best to leave as they are.

At the node content type level, it's required to configure the display format of the Image field. By default, this uses the Image field formatter and we never changed that, so it displays the picture using one of the default media styles. Navigate to **Structure | Content Types | rezepi | manage display** (`/admin/structure/types/manage/rezepi/display`) where we need to let Drupal know that we're interested in using the colorbox image formatter. For the **Picture** field, change the **FORMAT** column option to **Colorbox**, which will yield a change in the formatter configuration settings. Click on the rightmost, grey colored, gear icon to update these settings. For the **Content** image style one should probably set a small form size of the image, one of the existing thumbnail or medium image styles should do it, depending on your preference. For the **Colorbox** image style one should probably set a bigger image style as this will be the image that will show up in the lightbox pop up. I've gone with **None** (original image), which obviously shows the original uploaded image.

To confirm the result works as expected, edit the Kubbeh Soup content or create a new one and make sure the picture field is indeed populated with an image (which should be the case as we've made it a required field previously). Then visit the node and notice how the image shows up in a small thumbnail form. If you click on it, the lightbox should pop up and show the image in a bigger size, as you selected.

 The Colorbox formatter allows for more configurations such as supporting multiple images attached to a node. The **Gallery** setting defines the lightbox behavior in the case where multiple images are set for the node, such as enabling slideshow functionality to navigate across the node's images, instead of clicking and closing them one by one. Furthermore, the **Caption** setting defines the source to use for the image title.

Colorbox for WYSIWYG integration

As we've seen earlier, providing proper WYSIWYG support greatly affects the productivity of users. The problem with adding an Image field is that pictures get separated from the node's text, and thus disconnect from the context of the content item's text. This is something we have been through before and we solved it by integrating the extra media button into the WYSIWYG toolbar. Yet the problem remains that these images that we add do not benefit from the lightbox pop-up effect, so the user needs to fine-tune their width and height settings to fit the text as well as the image.

With the addition of the colorbox library to Drupal, it's possible to utilize the library and get this to work manually by setting up the HTML `<img>` element with the correct attribute settings. Let's see how this works before we find better alternatives. Heading back to the Kubbeh Soup content item we can see that apart from the Image field, the node's body field is using the WYSIWYG editor on full HTML text format and also embeds an image in the text, which does absolutely nothing if you click on it:

Even without integrating any third-party modules, it's possible at this point to make lightbox work for that image. To do this, we need to address the following items:

- Set the **URL** field in the **Link** tab to point to the original image
- Set the CSS class to also contain colorbox

With that in mind, we will edit the Kubbeh Soup node and double-click on the image in the **Recipe** field (or right-click on it and choose **Image Properties**). Copy the URL in the first **Image Info** tab and paste it into the **URL** field of the **Link** tab with a slight modification; we're interested in showing up the original image in the lightbox pop up so it's required to clean up that URL a bit and remove the `/styles/thumbnail/public/` segments so that it looks something like `/sites/default/files/picture.png`. Click on **Ok** in the **Image Properties** dialog and then reopen it. Navigate to the **Advanced** tab and in the **Stylesheet Classes** field, add **colorbox** and click on **Ok**. Save the node and watch how it's possible now to click on the image and display it in its original size using the lightbox effect.

This obviously results in a poor user experience, and there are better ways of achieving this goal, one of which is the popular Insert module. It attaches to the Image fields and after uploading an image it simply adds an **insert** button, which when clicked injects the required HTML `<img>` tag into a text area, where the cursor mark is. The problem with the Insert module is that it has no support for the Media module and only works with the Image fields where the widget is Image too (and not Media file selector). Then, there's the Media Colorbox module (`http://drupal.org/project/media_colorbox`), which might prove to be a better candidate for cross modules Media and Colorbox integration, but at this point it's not mature enough to provide proper WYSIWYG support and definitely has some bugs.

Installing colorbox

Download the Media Colorbox module's 7.x development version (`http://drupal.org/project/media_colorbox`) and install it. The module aims to simply add colorbox field formatters for the **Image** file type so we just need to set that up first.

Navigate to **Structure | File Types | Image | manage file display** (`/admin/structure/file-types/manage/audio/file-display`) where you should see that there's already a Media Colorbox enabled display. Configure it and adjust the **File view** mode to **Teaser**, the **Colorbox** view mode to **Preview**, and **Gallery** to **No gallery**. Add an **Image** display and set the **Image style** field to **None** (original image). With regards to the **Display** precedence order setting, make sure that the **Image** display is first and the **Media Colorbox** display is second.

In the **Teaser** mode of the file display (`/admin/structure/file-types/manage/audio/file-display/teaser`) make sure that the **Image** display is the only one enabled, and set the **Image style** field to **thumbnail**. Similar to that, we'll need to set up the **Colorbox** mode of the file display (`/admin/structure/file-types/manage/audio/file-display/colorbox`) and set **Gallery** to **No gallery** too (the first and second fields should be left set to **Default**).

We're ready to try this out. Let's edit the **rezepi** node and add a picture using the **Media Browser** button on the WYSIWYG toolbar. After choosing one of the images there and clicking on **Submit**, the following screen should appear, in which we should now change the current format to **Colorbox**; click on **Submit** and then save the node:

The lightbox effect should now show up for the selected images from the WYSIWYG toolbar. Support for this may still have its bugs and if you're not planning to use the Media file selector widget, then one can use another module called Insert which does the job well and is very simple to install too.

Colorbox for views

We can also benefit from the colorbox functionality easily in views.

It requires a simple change in the Image field formatter for existing views, so let's pick up the Recent Memos view (`/recent-memos`) that we created earlier. You can either find it by navigating to **Structure | Views** (`/admin/structure/views`), or if you navigate directly to it via the URL or menu entry that we added, just click on the rightmost gear icon and choose the **Edit** view.

In the **FIELDS** section click on the field called **Content: Image**, which will open the configuration screen for this field in a new pop-up window. For the **Formatter** field set the **Colorbox** option, for the **Content** image style choose **thumbnail**, for the **Colorbox** image style choose **None** (original image), and for **Gallery** choose **No gallery**.

Click on **Apply** and then save the view. Now when images are clicked upon, the lightbox effect will kick-in.

Multiple file uploads

We've been using the Media module as a very integral part of building our rich media content website, and while it does provide a rich user experience, it has its shortcomings, and it's not a full blown solution.

We will examine how to add multiple files upload support across a Drupal website, thus providing better user experience for site builders as well as the site's user audience.

Multiple file uploads for site administrators

When we are mostly dealing with user experience and functionality, it's easy to forget the fact that you, the site builder and administrator, are a user too and should also benefit from better experience.

As site administrators we are able to upload media by navigating to **Content** | **Files** (`/admin/content/file`) and adding files to our site's media library, but clicking on the **Add file** link would only allow us to upload files one by one.

To resolve that, we can make use of the plupload library and its Drupal integration module. For the library, surf over to `http://www.plupload.com/download.php` and download the GPLv2 version. Extract it into `sites/all/libraries`, which should result in `sites/all/libraries/plupload/js/plupload.full.js` being accessible.

For the Drupal module, we will download the Plupload integration module (`http://drupal.org/project/plupload`), which is used by other modules too to provide a better file upload experience. Once downloaded and enabled, the functionality should already be provided.

Let's navigate back to **Content | Files** and click on **Add file** again. If the installation was successful we should see a form like the one shown in the following screenshot, which allows for drag-and-drop as well as multiple file selection:

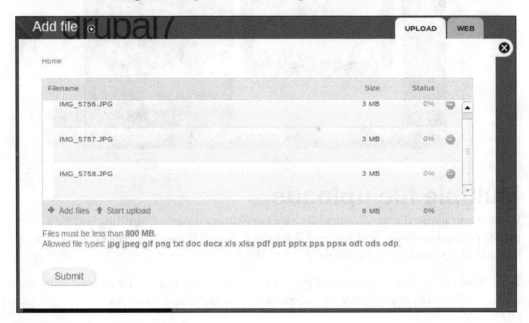

Multiple file uploads for user's Image fields

Providing a similar functionality for single nodes requires that we work with either the File or Image field types and with a dedicated upload widget based on the plupload integration.

To meet this requirement we will need two additional modules: Multiupload Filefield Widget (`http://drupal.org/project/multiupload_filefield_widget`) and Multiupload Imagefield Widget (`http://drupal.org/project/multiupload_imagefield_widget`). Download and install both modules (note that the former is a required module which the Imagefield widget module builds upon).

Because we mentioned this upload functionality affects the File and Image type fields let's work with the Memo content type that we created earlier, which uses the Image field. Navigate to **Structure | Content types | Memo | Manage fields** (`/admin/structure/types/manage/memo/fields`) and you should see that the Image field we added makes use of an Image field type as well as an Image widget. To change this widget, click on the **Image** link (of the **WIDGET** column), change the **Widget type** setting to **Multiupload**, and then click on **Continue**.

We will also need to edit the Image field's settings (`/admin/structure/types/manage/memo/fields/field_image`) and make sure that the **Number of values** setting has the **Unlimited** option selected (or another value greater than one obviously).

Finally, save this node field's settings and proceed to editing an existing Memo content type or creating a new one. At first, the upload widget may look the same as before, but notice that you can actually select multiple files in the system files dialog.

After selecting the files you can either save the node or click on the **Upload** button to see the uploaded files information before you save.

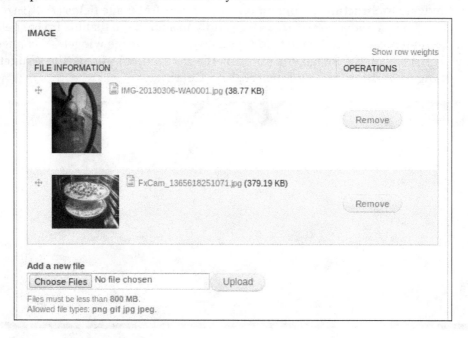

Extending image style effects

Earlier in this chapter we've seen how basic image effects can be applied to pictures that users upload. We will introduce a new module now that will help us in further extending the effects pool available for users on a Drupal website.

The module in question is called ImageCache Actions, which originates from earlier Drupal versions where this functionality was referred to as ImageCache. Proceed to download (http://drupal.org/project/imagecache_actions) and install it. Notice that this module comes bundled with a bunch of other modules that should be enabled too: ImageCache Canvas Actions and ImageCache Color Actions.

You may wonder what's the point in adding image effects? What is there to it? I'll then remind you of Instagram, a company whose entire product delivery was to enable users to take pictures from their smartphone and apply basic image effects to them. By the way, they recently also added a web application to accompany their mobile app product offering.

The module offers quite a handful of image manipulation options to choose from and build on. We will go about adding two image style presets to set an example of how to make use of the module.

Navigate to **Configuration | Media | Image Styles** (`/admin/config/media/image-styles`) and add a new image style called `effect_reddish`. Apply the following effects:

- **Rounded corners**: Set the radius to **100**
- **Color shift**: Set the hex value to **FF0000**

This should result in an effect similar to the following screenshot:

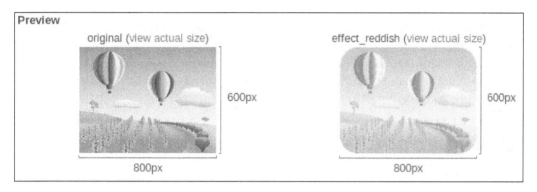

If you're satisfied save this image style or continue tweaking it at your will.

Proceeding to our next example, we will make use of an existing image as a watermark on uploaded images. For the watermark effect, we need to specify the path of the image that we will use as the watermark image in Drupal's filesystem (such as a logo or a signature). From the previous chapters, we can make use of the DigiDoc pictures as an example here to add signatures to images in our website. If you decide to do so, then just find the filename for it. Otherwise, you can upload a new image by navigating to **Content | Files** (`/file/add`) and directly uploading it there.

Create another image style and name it `effect_watermark`, and add the Overlay (watermark) effect to it. For the **X Offset** field set **right**, for the **Y Offset** field set **top**. While it's possible to use numeric values, using terms such as top right to set the watermark position is easier and more convenient. Set **Opacity** to **100** and for the **filename** field use the format `public://picture.png` to specify the image you will be using, which indicates that the `picture.png` image we are interested in using should be found in the `public` filesystem folder in Drupal.

If you're not satisfied with the results in the preview you can change positions or possibly consider changing an image for one that better suits a watermark. The end result should look similar to the following screenshot:

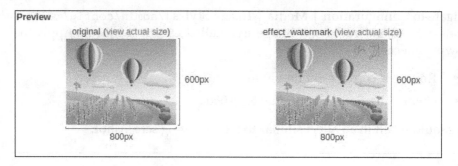

There are many more effects that can be created just with those set of configuration options that the ImageCache Actions module provides, and one can come up with more than just an Instagram-clone idea for your next web or mobile ventures, one for example is a greeting card application.

Adding your own effects with custom modules

If you are pursuing a project which requires a great deal of image manipulation, chances are that you will not find all of this functionality in contributed modules, and that's ok. It's expected that third-party modules will give you an immediate solution for better **time-to-market** (**TTM**), and from there on Drupal's immensely modular and flexible architecture will allow you to use its facilities to create your own modules.

Drupal's workflow for implementing an image effect is simple and is as follows. Once an image effect has been declared using the appropriate hook, it is served as a callback function when an effect needs to be applied. When that occurs, the callback should invoke an image toolkit (as there may be more than one and it depends on operating systems and installs, such as whether the library is installed or not), which applies the appropriate effect implementation and returns the image object.

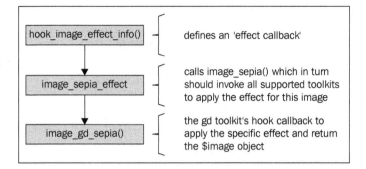

To achieve this image effect add-on, we will create our own module code to implement an image sepia tone effect. A sepia tone, which you probably have seen on image related applications such as Instagram, is a picture that has been manipulated to make use of colors in the brown range tone, which ultimately gives it a style of old photographs.

Without diving too much into graphics theory we will simply point out that a certain color can be represented in many ways, one of which is the hexadecimal notation which is widely and most popularly used around the Web today, for example #00FF00. The same color can also be represented in its red, green, and blue tone strength. For our image effect, red, brown, yellow, gold, all with the proper color tone can be referred to as sepia. There is no one RGB code that is to be used, but rather one can decide upon the desired values to create the shade of brown that is most appropriate.

What color is #00FF00? When specifying a color in hexadecimal notation we can split it in three equal parts, in our example, 00, FF, and 00.
Each part maps to its equivalent red, green, and blue component. Each component is made up of a byte, so if the notation is hex, its range is from 00 and upwards to FF. If the decimal system is used to note in RGB style, it ranges from 0 to 255, resulting in 256 color options for each component. Because we have three components of 256 colors, this adds up to 256 * 256 * 256 = 16,777,216 possible colors that can be specified. Understanding the color system, we can look into our #00FF00 example. Because 00 is used for the red and blue components we know that there will be no such color tone of either. We are now left with green, specified in FF, which is equivalent to 255; it is now clear that #00FF00 is simply a green color.

To begin with our module, we need to create the module's directory and files structure. Name the directory `image_effect_sepia`, create the directory `sites/all/modules/image_effect_sepia`, and our first file `sites/all/modules/image_effect_sepia/image_effect_sepia.info`, which will be used as our module's metadata information for Drupal. Its content is as follows:

```
name = "Image Effect - Sepia"
description = "Adds a Sepia image effect to image styles"
core = 7.x
files[] = image_effect_sepia.module
```

Proceed to create the actual module's code in the module file `sites/all/modules/image_effect_sepia/image_effect_sepia.module`. The code that we will use in this module is stripped down to simply the hooks we need to implement for the image effect just as we described the process in the flow chart previously:

```php
<?php

/**
 * @file
 * Functions implementing the image effects hooks to provide a Sepia
   color effect
 */

/**
 * Implements hook_image_effect_info().
 */
function image_effect_sepia_image_effect_info() {

  $effects = array(
    'image_sepia' => array(
      'label' => t('Sepia'),
      'help' => t('Sepia converts an image to old images look,
        kinda brown-ish.'),
      'effect callback' => 'image_sepia_effect',
      'dimensions passthrough' => TRUE,
    ),
  );

  return $effects;

}

/**
```

```
 * Image effect callback; Sepia effect of an image resource.
 *
 * @param $image
 * An image object returned by image_load().
 * @param $data
 * An array of attributes to use when performing the sepia effect.
 * @return
 * TRUE on success. FALSE on failure to turn image to sepia.
 */
function image_effect_sepia_image_sepia_effect(&$image, $data) {

  if (!image_sepia($image)) {

    watchdog('image', 'Image sepia failed using the %toolkit
      toolkit on %path (%mimetype, %dimensions)',
      array('%toolkit' => $image->toolkit, '%path' =>
      $image->source, '%mimetype' => $image->info['mime_type'],
      '%dimensions' => $image->info['width'] . 'x' .
      $image->info['height']), WATCHDOG_ERROR);
    return FALSE;
  }
  return TRUE;

}


/**
 * Our own call back for applying the image effect which will
   invoke any image toolkit's libraries that implement this
   sepia color effect
 *
 * @param $image
 * An image object returned by image_load().
 */
function image_sepia(stdClass $image) {
  return image_toolkit_invoke('sepia', $image);
}
```

Moving on to create our image effect we will be making use of the API provided by PHP's GD library (http://php.net/manual/en/book.image.php), which is quite simple and straightforward. Let's review some examples of general use, where to begin with, we need to create an image object, which we can either do from scratch, or from an existing image as follows:

```
// New image created, specifying its size:
$width = $height = 400;
$image = imagecreate($width, $height);
```

```
// An image object created from an existing image, specifying its
   filename
$image = imagecreatefrompng($file_path);
```

With the `$image` object, we can then apply one of the many image manipulation functions that the GD library exposes for us. When working with a new image object, we can set the background color by using `imagecolorallocate()`, and recursively use it again to create a color using RGB values, for example:

```
// This will set the background color to red for initial images that
   were created with imagecreate()
$red = imagecolorallocate ($image, 255, 0, 0);
```

There are many more functions for you to explore such as writing text, creating shapes, and employing color manipulations.

For our Sepia effect, we will make use of the `imagefilter()` function, which receives an `$image` object to work on, an image filter type, and optional arguments for setting the RGB values.

```
/**
 * Convert an image to sepia color tone
 *
 * @param $image
 * An image object. The $image->resource value will be modified by
   this call.
 * @return
 * TRUE or FALSE, based on success.
 *
 */
function image_effect_sepia_image_gd_sepia(stdClass $image) {

  // PHP installations using non-bundled GD do not have imagefilter.
  if (!function_exists('imagefilter')) {
    watchdog('image', 'The image %file could not be applied the
      sepia effect because the imagefilter() function is not
      available in this PHP installation.', array('%file' =>
      $image->source));
    return FALSE;
  }

  imagefilter($image->resource, IMG_FILTER_GRAYSCALE);
  return imagefilter($image->resource, IMG_FILTER_COLORIZE, 150,
    50, 0);

}
```

As you can see, before applying the brownish color tone we first apply the grayscale image filter, which turns the image into black and white by calculating each pixel's intensity, and then apply the brownscale colors tone using the `IMG_FILTER_COLORIZE` filter.

Save the module file and we are now ready to enable it. To watch it in action you can navigate to the **Image Styles** configuration (`admin/config/media/image-styles`), create a new image style, and apply the **Sepia** effect to it.

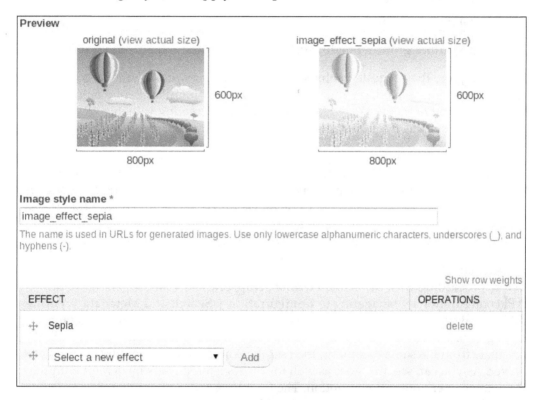

Enabling rating of content

Throughout this chapter we've seen how it's possible to extend the functionality of media assets, primarily images, and user experience when handling them. We have even covered how to customize this experience using our own module code.

Let's not forget that there are other ways to enhance overall media content with functionality and features which do not surround the actual media handling. There are many examples of this, such as:

- Enabling comments to stir discussion amongst your web applications' community

- Enabling the use of hash-tags or @ symbols to mention users, so that visitors get hooked to your website, and are encouraged to stay longer

- Enabling the rating of content

The list can further grow depending on your use case and imagination.

We will explore the suggested enhancement of enabling users to rate the content, specifically media related, on your website. It is a very popular feature amongst social collaboration networks, which sets the path on creating valuable views as a site builder such as popular and suggested content by your users and most active users.

To add this feature, we will use the Fivestar Drupal module, which leverages for this purpose some other Drupal dependencies and JavaScript libraries. To begin, we will need to download and enable the 7.x branch version of the following modules:

- Fivestar (`http://drupal.org/project/fivestar`)

- Voting API (`http://drupal.org/project/votingapi`)

Before proceeding with the actual Fivestar setup, one can visit the general Voting API configuration by navigating to **Configuration | Search and Metadata | Voting API** (`/admin/config/search/votingapi`) and make any changes to the default settings. For example, if you wish to count anonymous votes as one vote, even if they originate from the same computer, then set the **Anonymous vote rollover** setting to **Never**. As you can see, this goes as well for the registered users by default with the **Registered user vote rollover** option. The final **Vote tallying** option refers to the time when the calculation of all votes should take place to provide the final results. The default is probably fairly sane if you're just starting off.

 To enable anonymous users to cast votes on nodes, you might need to adjust the permissions at `/admin/people/permissions` with the **rate** content permission for the anonymous user role.

The Fivestar rating module can be used in numerous ways, either enabling it using the fields configuration for a node content type, or by developers making use of its API. Its general configuration is quite simple, and allows you to enable several voting per content type if required. Navigate to Fivestar's configuration page at **Configuration | Content Authoring | Fivestar** (/admin/config/content/fivestar) and apply the voting tags name, which is used to specify the voting categories. On most occasions, the voting is per node content type, so we will be leaving this as the default option and click on **Save configuration**.

Adding a rating field for content types

Let's add a rating field for the Concertz content type. Navigate to **Structure | Content types | Concertz | Manage fields** (/admin/structure/types/manage/concertz/fields) and add a new field called **Rating**. Choose the **Fivestar** rating for the **FIELD TYPE** setting and for the **WIDGET TYPE** setting choose the first option **Stars** (rated while viewing). The **WIDGET TYPE** option defines the behavior of the voting widget, such as whether users are allowed to vote when the node is being viewed or edited, and whether we would like to use a drop-down select list instead of the rating icons. In most cases it's probably desired to allow users to cast their vote when they view the node, hence the first option for this setting is our choice, **Stars** (rated while viewing). After clicking on the **Save** button we get forwarded, as usual, to the settings page, where we can set the following:

- The **Number of stars** field allows you to set the amount of star icons that should be drawn and serves as the highest vote that can be specified for the node

- Allow users to cancel their vote at any point in time after voting

- The **Rating field settings** field, if it is required to maintain multiple votes in separate categories, helps you to specify the vote category using taxonomy tags

Once you are satisfied with those settings click on the **Save settings** button.

The Fivestar module ships with several widgets that one can use to display the voting icons, and of course enables developers to extend with their own widgets. The voting widget hosts more than just formatting, so we will navigate to **MANAGE DISPLAY** (/admin/structure/types/manage/concertz/display) now to examine the possible configuration allowed for this widget.

For the display format, aside from the interactive icons option, the **Rating** and **Percentage** options are pretty straightforward. They will either show a 4/5 text or a 80 percent plain text output, respectively. The more interesting and common use of the Fivestar module formatting is the **Stars** view.

After choosing the **As Stars** setting, click on the gray gear icon on the right-hand side of the page and notice that you can choose from quite a few options for drawing the stars icon:

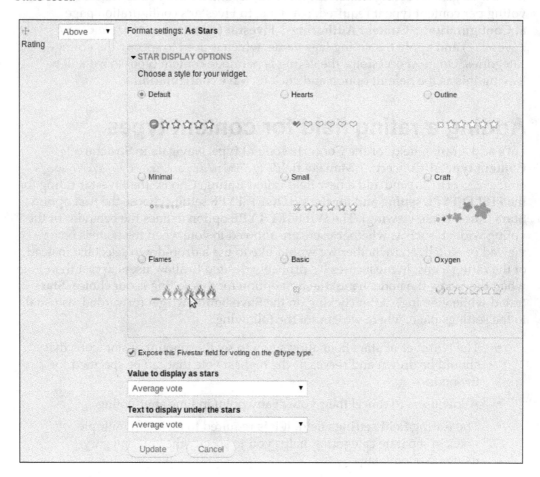

Aside from the actual icons for the look and feel, this display format allows us to configure whether to display the average vote or the user's own vote, as well as tune the stars text display.

> If you wish to further enhance the user's feedback regarding content on your website there are other modules which extend the Voting API such as Plus1 and Is Useful.

Once you have updated this format with your desired settings, make sure you save it and navigate to one of the Concertz content types that we created earlier. It should look like the following screenshot:

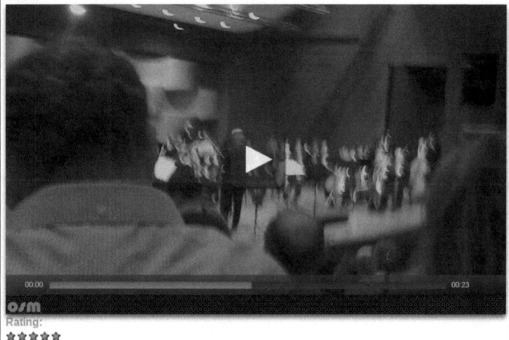

Summary

In this chapter we reviewed Drupal's media configuration and tools which aid a site builder in enhancing media-related content. With image styles, we learned how to apply image manipulations and how to build our own effects. For better user experience we explored the use of Colorbox and Plupload modules. Finally, we learned about the rating module, which adds voting capabilities.

In the next chapter we will take a tour of the upcoming and promising Drupal 8 version, where we will explore new features that it brings and how we should prepare for it as site builders.

9
Drupal 8 and Beyond

This chapter will explore the upcoming Drupal 8 release and its overall changes and features, and review what awaits for website builders in this next revolutionary release.

In this chapter, we will cover:

- Introduction to Drupal 8
- Drupal 8 tour guide

Introduction to Drupal 8

If you are familiar with Drupal's release lifecycle, then you should know that there are always two versions. The officially released and stable version, in our case this is Drupal 7, which is kept up to date with any bugs or security patches required so it is fully supported. Once Drupal 7 was officially released, developers were able to start focusing their efforts on implementing their next version of a brand new and shining Drupal.

This upcoming version of Drupal 8 is as revolutionary as any of the earlier major releases.

If you would like to get your copy of the latest version of Drupal 8 then you'd need to set up git (http://git-scm.com), the distributed version control system, and get a copy of the Drupal repository. From command line, you can simply run git clone http://git.drupal.org/project/drupal.git, which will create a drupal/ directory in the current directory tree. As it is with git, you'd be getting the entire repository with all branches that were created so you can also easily switch through any of them. You can find more instructions on using git with Drupal at https://drupal.org/project/drupal/git-instructions.

Drupal 8 architecture changes

Drupal 8's core initiatives are organized around topics, with assigned team members and team leaders to help carry out the objectives. Each core initiative aims to focus on a topic which Drupal, hopes to improve on, and bridge the gap with the current demand for advanced web applications. The initiatives for Drupal 8 are:

- Configuration management
- HTML5
- Layouts
- Mobile
- Multilingual
- Views in core
- Web services

You can probably relate to most of these topics and understand why Drupal needs to provide better support in each area. HTML5, mobile, and views should not be strangers to you as we have learned about them in the context of Drupal throughout this book.

Other topics such as **Configuration Management Initiative (CMI)** have been addressed due to the problem of separation of configuration from data. Drupal developers would easily relate to this pain because everything in Drupal is kept in the database, whether it's module's configuration and general settings or actual data payload like users. In such a design, it is very hard to manage different Drupal instances which share the same data (the state of the database) but not the same configuration. For example, you can think of development lifecycle which requires a test server, a staging server, and a production server.

Integration with Symfony2

While Drupal is a very advanced **Content Management System (CMS)** and even somewhat of a framework too (CMF), it is still not employing design patterns or architecture design, which is stopping it from being up-to-date with current technology advancements.

Drupal 8 has decided to adopt and make use of Symfony2 components in order to meet design requirements for its internal structure, without having to reinvent the wheel. Some of these components are HttpKernel, Routing, EventDispatcher, DependencyInjection, ClassLoader, and others all of which will aid Drupal by using high quality code-base that has been tested by the very large Symfony community, and now pairing it with Drupal will even allow for more improvements.

 Symfony2 (http://www.symfony.com) is an open source, enterprise-grade PHP framework for web development by SensioLabs. It provides a handful of components for web application development, which are decoupled and reusable, making it an obvious option for other PHP applications and frameworks to leverage these set of libraries.

One of the benefits of integrating Symfony2 components is that Drupal's very unique design structure and development model hinders on new comers who find it difficult to understand. By integrating with Symfony2 components, it introduces familiar programming concepts that developers coming from other frameworks have already learned. Moreover, it provides the ability to easily leverage shared libraries across developers in the eco system, especially with the establishment of the **PHP Framework Interoperability Group (PHP-FIG)**.

Release timeline and when to expect Drupal 8

You're probably wondering when should we expect Drupal 8 to be released and how soon can we migrate to it if we wanted to.

While code freeze was originally planned for April 2013, its current due date is probably more along the lines of July 2013, which shortly after Drupal 8 will be officially released. How long after July, no one knows exactly (it was planned for September 2013 originally) but it will happen once there are no release-critical issues pending in the queue. We can estimate due to experience with previous releases that this time frame would be around two to six months.

Although, even if Drupal 8 will be released by December 2013 this isn't really translating to any immediate actions when as site builders will delay in adopting this new release due to architecture changes and the lack of modules support in this new version. Developers will probably take some time until they fully grasp the new internal design of Drupal 8 and catch up with the learning curve to complete their versions for it.

As we can see in the usage chart per Drupal version (which you can always follow up on for more updates on `https://drupal.org/project/usage/drupal`), while Drupal 7 was released around January 2011 it only surpassed site builders adoption more than a year later at around April 2012.

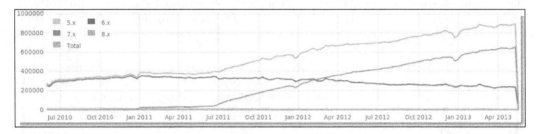

Drupal's release cycle visualized by Dries Buytart (`http://buytaert.net/drupal-8-feature-freeze-extended`) shows the actions that take place in each phase of the development lifecycle and will help you figure out what to expect accordingly:

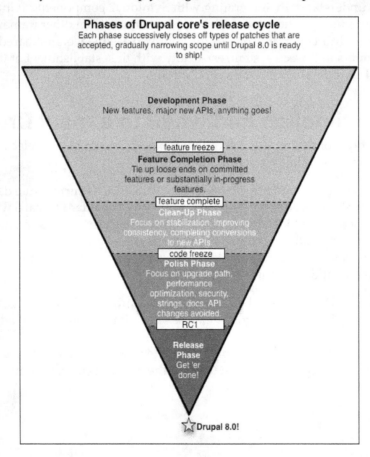

Drupal 8 tour guide

Once you've loaded up Drupal 8's installer in the browser you will see that it is pretty much the same as Drupal 7, in terms of UI as well as installation options where you can choose different install profiles and setup database configuration.

When the installation process is finished, Drupal's landing page looks as follows, and you will immediately notice that the administrative toolbar has been shrunken to take up less space.

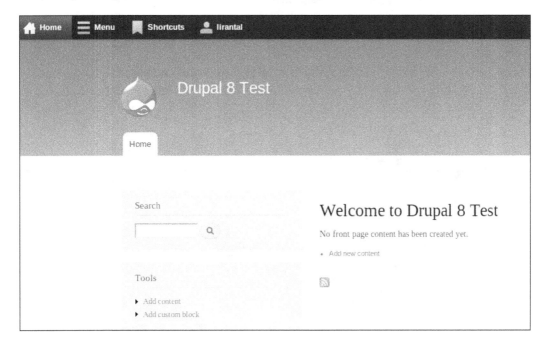

Another important aspect of theming that you can immediately notice is that the default theme has been made responsive from the ground up and now, loading up your Drupal website from a mobile device will actually render into a usable user interface. The administrative tool bar menu items have been stripped out of their descriptive texts and the overall layout has shifted into a single column view to make sure everything fits into the screen.

Another layout related change that we can notice in the landing page is the contextual editor. By clicking on the right-most pencil icon that shows up on the administrative tool bar at the top, all the blocks, views, content, and any other Drupal element in the layout will immediately display the pencil icon wrapped around a rectangular container that will enable the respective contextual links. For example, on a block item we would be able to configure block settings, and for a view we'd be able to quickly edit the view.

This isn't a newly introduced functionality on its own but it has been streamlined now and it is setting the grounds for in-place editing, which will greatly improve content editors' user experience.

If you are wondering how much emphasis has been put on providing a better experience for content editors, take a look at the page for creating a new article:

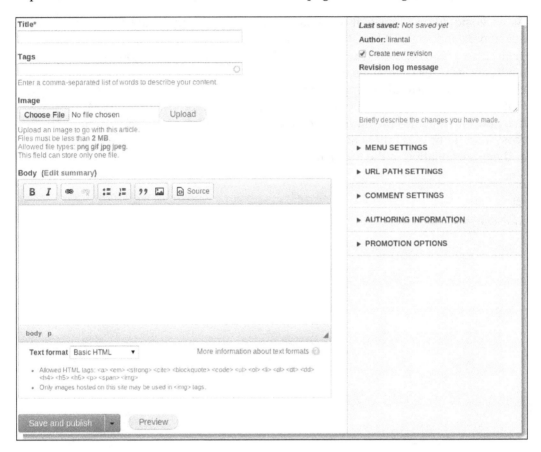

The vertical tabbed options which we've seen in earlier Drupal versions were moved to the right side of the screen in its own column. It resembles WordPress (http://www.wordpress.com), the popular blog publishing system, quite a bit and it genuinely looks cleaner. More importantly maybe, we can see that the WYSIWYG editor CKEditor that we've been working with throughout this book is the default and built-in content editor in Drupal 8.

Summary

We have reviewed the upcoming Drupal 8 release and the changes it is introducing. Many of those changes are architecture and software design related changes such as configuration management, core framework refactoring, better layout, and general mobile-ready with built-in support for HTML5.

As we've noted previously, it will take some time for Drupal 8 to be adopted by developers and site builders. While the media initiative group (`https://groups.drupal.org/media/media-initiative`) has been working hard on providing better media support for Drupal, as we've seen with the Media module throughout this book, there are currently no products to work with for Drupal 8, nor is there any built-in support for proper media handling as we covered in this book. Moreover, there are currently no media management related modules on Drupal's modules ecosystem (to be exact there are only six modules in the media category and none of them is of relation to the topics in our book).

Index

E

entities 10-12
EventDispatcher 229
Evernote
  URL 12

F

FCKeditor 65
FedEx 7
fields
  about 18
  adding, to memo content type 19-23
File entity
  URL 51
filesystem configuration 200
Fivestar module
  URL 222

G

GD Graphics Library 200
General Public License (GNU) 7
getID3 Drupal module
  downloading 159
  installing 160
  URL 159
getID3 library
  installing 159
graphical charts
  used, for visualizing data 182, 183

H

Highcharts
  URL 184
HTML4 83
HTML5
  about 83
  basic page skeleton 84, 85
  canvas 90-92
  data, visualizing with graphical charts 182, 183
  features 83-85
  form elements 86
  media 87-89
  Microdata 177
  RDFa 173
  real-world examples 172
  resources 92
  responsive web design 192
HTML5 Canvas Cookbook
  URL 93
HTML5, in Drupal 93
HTML5 markup 88
HTML5 media player
  installing 125, 126
HTML5 Multimedia Development
  URL 93
HTML5 Tools module 93-97
HTML5 Web Application Development by example
  URL 93
HttpKernel 229

I

ID3 module 158
ID3 PHP library
  about 158
  downloading 159
  installing 159
ImageCache 201
  about 214
  URL 214
ImageCache Canvas Actions 214
ImageCache Color Actions 214
image galleries
  about 72
  blocks, creating 80, 81
  creating 74-79
ImageMagick 200
image style effects
  color shift 215
  custom effects, adding 216-221
  extending 214, 215
  rounded corners 215
  watermark effect 215
image styles
  about 201

Thank you for buying
Drupal 7 Media

About Packt Publishing

Packt, pronounced 'packed', published its first book "*Mastering phpMyAdmin for Effective MySQL Management*" in April 2004 and subsequently continued to specialize in publishing highly focused books on specific technologies and solutions.

Our books and publications share the experiences of your fellow IT professionals in adapting and customizing today's systems, applications, and frameworks. Our solution based books give you the knowledge and power to customize the software and technologies you're using to get the job done. Packt books are more specific and less general than the IT books you have seen in the past. Our unique business model allows us to bring you more focused information, giving you more of what you need to know, and less of what you don't.

Packt is a modern, yet unique publishing company, which focuses on producing quality, cutting-edge books for communities of developers, administrators, and newbies alike. For more information, please visit our website: www.packtpub.com.

About Packt Open Source

In 2010, Packt launched two new brands, Packt Open Source and Packt Enterprise, in order to continue its focus on specialization. This book is part of the Packt Open Source brand, home to books published on software built around Open Source licences, and offering information to anybody from advanced developers to budding web designers. The Open Source brand also runs Packt's Open Source Royalty Scheme, by which Packt gives a royalty to each Open Source project about whose software a book is sold.

Writing for Packt

We welcome all inquiries from people who are interested in authoring. Book proposals should be sent to author@packtpub.com. If your book idea is still at an early stage and you would like to discuss it first before writing a formal book proposal, contact us; one of our commissioning editors will get in touch with you.

We're not just looking for published authors; if you have strong technical skills but no writing experience, our experienced editors can help you develop a writing career, or simply get some additional reward for your expertise.

Drupal 7 Development by Example Beginner's Guide

ISBN: 978-1-84951-680-8   Paperback: 366 pages

Follow the creation of a Drupal website to learn, by example, the key concepts of Drupal 7 development and HTML5

1. A hands-on, example-driven guide to programming Drupal websites

2. Discover a number of new features for Drupal 7 through practical and interesting examples while building a fully functional recipe sharing website

3. Learn about web content management, multi-media integration, and e-commerce in Drupal 7

Drupal 7 Themes

ISBN: 978-1-84951-276-3   Paperback: 320 pages

Create new themes for your Drupal 7 site with a clean layout and powerful CSS styling

1. Learn to create new Drupal 7 themes

2. No experience of Drupal theming required

3. Discover techniques and tools for creating and modifying themes

4. The first book to guide you through the new elements and themes available in Drupal 7

Please check **www.PacktPub.com** for information on our titles

Drupal 7 Business Solutions

ISBN: 978-1-84951-664-8   Paperback: 378 pages

Build powerful website features for your business

1. Build a Drupal 7 powered website for your business rapidly

2. Add blogs, news, e-commerce, image galleries, maps, surveys, polls, and forums to your website to beat competition

3. Complete example of a real world site with clear explanation

Drupal 7 Cookbook

ISBN: 978-1-84951-796-6   Paperback: 324 pages

Over 70 recipes that will advance your Drupal skills from novice to pro

1. Install, set up, and manage a Drupal site and discover how to get the most out of creating and displaying content

2. Become familiar with creating new content types and use them to create and publish content using Views, Blocks, and Panels

4. Learn how to work with images, documents, and video and how to integrate them with Facebook, Twitter, and Add this

Please check **www.PacktPub.com** for information on our titles